What We Owe to Ourselves

Also by Nicole Antoinette

How To Be Alone:
an 800-mile hike on the Arizona Trail

What We Owe to Ourselves

A 500-mile hike on the Colorado Trail

Nicole Antoinette

Paperback ISBN: 979-8-9870971-2-0
eBook ISBN: 979-8-9870971-3-7

*For anyone who has ever had an unlikely dream—
a wish, a goal, a desire to change their life—and who
was brave enough to look themselves in the eye
and say: "Why not me?"*

Meet The Hikers

NICOLE ANTOINETTE
(aka Tinkerbell, aka Tink,
aka the person telling this story)

Pronouns: she/her

Age: 36

Trail resume:
I started long-distance hiking in 2016, setting off alone on the 460-mile Oregon section of the Pacific Crest Trail with no prior backpacking experience (oops!), a trek during which I cried pretty much every day (fun!) and at the end of it I made a big loud declaration about never wanting to hike another step ever again no matter what.

2017: Ignored said declaration and committed committed to trying again, this time on the 800-mile Arizona Trail in late fall when there was very little water and an abundance of sharp and venomous things; somehow completed this hike over the course of 44 days, a story which is chronicled in my previous trail memoir, *How To Be Alone.*

2018: Attempted a southbound thru-hike of the Pacific Crest Trail; quit a little after the halfway point (87 days and 1600 miles in); felt like a total failure for a while; questioned long-distance hiking and why a person would keep subjecting themselves to such a hard thing over and over again for no real reason.

2019, Part I: Got divorced—not as a direct result of long-distance hiking but not *not* because of it either. (Turns out that a relationship can be exceptionally challenging when one person wants to spend months of every year in the mountains and the other person does not, especially when combined with other in-compatibilities and divergent visions for the future).

2019, Part II: Hiked 700 more miles on the PCT immediately after moving out of the home I owned with my former spouse, and felt like I was drowning in sadness and a deep searing grief the whole time. I also experienced what happens when a person under-takes a long early spring hike after an entirely seden-tary winter of depression and zero training (PSA: do not recommend!)

2019, Part III: Built out and moved into a 20 square foot van; fell in love with someone else; drove across the country with him; saw the Colorado Trail for the first time and hiked along it for about an hour, just a quick jaunt out and back from a roadside trailhead but that was enough to light a flame of desire about coming back and trying to hike the whole trail next year.

2020: COVID-19 pandemic sweeps across the world; everything shuts down; Colorado Trail trek is cancelled.

March 2021: The one-year anniversary of the start of the pandemic; nothing is how it was before; getting divorced and changing my entire life so as to be able to travel and hike and live on the road is a dream that (because of the pandemic) has not yet been fully realized (is it even still the dream anymore? would 'settling down' and having some permanence and roots be better? at what age is it no longer a good idea to go adventuring off into the woods and mountains for months at a time?)

June 2021: Okay, I'm fully vaccinated now and the Colorado Trail hike is officially back on; 491 miles from Denver to Durango, a personal commitment to myself to try one more long distance hike as a last chance to see if this wild little lifestyle I've been fantasizing about for years and years is *really* worth all that needs to be sacrificed in order for me to have it.

Game on.

◁ ▷

TOM GROSSMITH
(aka Gentleman, aka Gent, aka my beloved partner)

Pronouns: he/him

Age: 28

Trail resume: Gent started long-distance hiking on the PCT in 2015 (at the tender lil age of 22), and had to quit an attempted 2,650 mile thru-hike after just 110 miles due to knee injury (heartbreaking!); he eventually rehabbed the knee and hiked the Vermont section of the Appalachian Trail that year instead.

2016: He flew back out to the PCT (once in love with the PCT, always in love with the PCT it turns out) and hiked another 200 miles of it; he also hiked the 100

Mile Wilderness on the AT in 3.5 days in the humid middle of summer on a sprained ankle while being swarmed by a billion mosquitos (oh the things we can do when we are young).

2017: Another 100 miles of the PCT plus the New York section of the AT.

2018: Went back to the PCT for another thru-hike attempt, this time headed southbound; met Tink (that's me!) on day 3 and hiked with her as part of a four-person trail family for three months; quit the hike after 1600 miles—totally burnt out both physically and emotionally (and filled with questions about whether a completed thru-hike will ever be possible for him after so many failed attempts).

2019: Joined Tink for 700 miles of the PCT.

2020: Yep, you guessed it, pandemic.

June 2021: Started training in earnest for the Colorado Trail, convinced that *this* will be the year that his longtime thru-hike dream finally comes true.

◁ ▷

IRIS RANKIN
(aka Bugbite, aka my soulmate friend)

Pronouns: they/them

Age: 31

Trail resume: Long time backpacker, first time long-distance hiker.

2004: Bugbite first started backpacking during a 10-day trip in the Colorado wilderness that was mandatory for new students at their small experiential high school. Nothing about this trip was ultralight. Their pack weighed 64 pounds, saddled on an average-sized 14-year-old. Bugbite shuffled at the back of the group the entire week and a half with blistered feet, hip bones in agony, craving cheeseburgers (which as a vegetarian they didn't even eat), convinced that backpacking was a thoroughly stupid activity.

2004-2008: They kept backpacking anyway. They joined the hiking club at school. They backpacked in the canyons of Utah and the Colorado mountains and even did their senior project backpacking in Yosemite. They came full circle by taking new students out on that same mandatory hiking trip, listening to them complain about the cheeseburgers they also wanted to eat.

2008-2018: Lived (and hiked) in Washington, Alaska, Montana, and back in Colorado, and always assumed they'd do a long-distance hike but never did.

2019: The year of queer awakening, ending a long relationship, moving to the PNW on a whim, meeting Tink in person for the first time, and deciding that next year it would finally be time to do the damn thing: a long-distance hike. Bring on the Colorado Trail with Tink and Gent!

2020: Colorado Trail trek is cancelled. Their dad dies at the end of May, and a week spent hiking a section of the Oregon PCT with Tink and Gent over the summer is the only time they feel even remotely okay.

August 2021: New pack on their back (weighing more like 20 pounds this time, not 60, thank goodness), and ready to hike across Colorado!

"Seize this opportunity while you have it;
you never know what the future will bring.
The difference between talking about it and doing it
is doing it."

—RUTH REICHL, *DELICIOUS!: A NOVEL*

August 1, 2021

Denver, CO

I wake up to find that my underwear, one of only two pairs that I have with me right now, is entirely soaked with blood.

Well. Okay then.

I get out of bed quietly, turning on the bathroom light in the otherwise dark hotel room and carefully stripping the underwear off so that I can try rinsing the blood out in the sink. I watch the water turn bright red as it splashes into the basin, and as I look down I realize that it's not just my underwear that's covered in blood, it's my inner thighs too.

I turn off the tap and wring the underwear out as best I can, laying it over the shower rod to dry a little bit before I need to put it back on. It's just past 6am now, which means that I have less than two hours to go until I'll be standing at the northern terminus of the Colorado Trail, taking my first steps of what will hopefully be a successful thru-hike wherein I will hike the entire trail, all 491 miles of it, end to end in one go. And so of course this is the moment that my body has decided to begin bleeding. I shake my head, rooting around in my small first aid kit for the ibuprofen I need to take right now if I have any chance of getting ahead of the intensely painful cramps that will soon be my uninvited hiking companion. I swallow three tablets, 600mg total, and assess the limited supply of tampons I've packed. With how heavily I seem to be bleeding right now (much more heavily than usual for some reason?) I don't think I have enough tampons to get me through this initial section of the hike, not before reaching the first town where we'll resupply, so I quickly add "stop and buy more tampons" to the pre-hike to-do list I've created in the Notes app on my phone.

That list now looks like this:
- Buy more tampons (the super absorbent ones instead of the regular ones, maybe?)
- Double check all my gear one more time (am I *positive* I have everything I need?)
- Pack all gear
- Test to see if the trail maps on my phone are downloaded for offline use
- Fill water bottles, add to side pockets of pack
- Text Mom
- Turn on autoresponder email
- HIKE HIKE HIKE!

Okay, I say to myself, *let's do this.*

I begin working through the list alongside my partner, Gent, and our friend, Bugbite, who are in the hotel room with me right now, tending to their own pre-hike preparations. "Gent" and "Bugbite" are their trail names, a fun little custom in the long-distance hiking community wherein a nickname is bestowed upon you by other people, usually based on something silly or ridiculous you've done, or perhaps just a standout part of your personality. Gent is short for Gentleman, a name he was given by other hikers on the Pacific Crest Trail in 2018 when he was a clean-shaven, soft-spoken, always polite 25-year-old wearing a blue and white button-up shirt. Bugbite's name is a result of a short backpacking trip the three of us took together last summer, during which they wound up with more mosquito bites on their body than I ever thought it was possible for one person to get without swelling up and dying. There were just *so many bites*, especially on their back (underneath where the backpack was covering, so like... how! how did the mosquitos even get under there?) and having all those bites so close together made it look, by the end of the week, as if each individual bite had somehow morphed into one giant, red, angry, super-bite. I shudder now, even thinking about it.

Bugbite and Gent finish packing up before me, not having had to wash any bloody limbs and undergarments, so they leave the room first, headed down to the hotel's small breakfast buffet. I put the final gear items into my pack and clip it shut, taking one more lap of the room to make sure we remembered everything, and then I too am making my way to the breakfast buffet, not at all hungry since my stomach is already full of the wild flapping feeling of my nervous pre-hike butterflies.

I hear the laughter before I turn the corner into the breakfast room, coming from Gent and Bugbite and our friend Ellie, who has kindly agreed to drive us to the trailhead at this early hour. I drop my pack, give Ellie a hug, and then wander along the food counter in search of something to eat that might calm these butterflies. I settle on oatmeal, orange juice, and earl grey tea, but none of it seems particularly appealing. I eat what I can though, knowing I'll need the energy, and the others do the same. Soon we're all buckled into Ellie's car, our packs in the trunk, making a detour to the grocery store so I can run in and buy a box of the biggest tampons I can find. After that it's a quick ride to the trailhead, waving goodbye to Ellie, and then we're finally standing there, all three of us gathering close together for a photo in front of the the large wooden sign that marks the northern terminus of the Colorado Trail, the beginning of our adventure, 491 miles to go.

I'm giddy as we start walking the flat six miles through Waterton Canyon, buzzing on the adrenaline rush that comes from finally getting started on the thing you've been planning and thinking about and dreaming of for years. Literally, years.

But am I actually ready for this, I wonder? I trained a decent amount over the summer, but I haven't hiked at all in the past two weeks, not even a single step. Have I lost my fitness? Is my body ready? Is my mind ready? Do I even remember how to pitch my tent? It's been over two years now since the end of my last long-distance hike, much of that time spent indoors in pandemic isolation, and it feels utterly surreal to finally be vaccinated and to be able to get back into this hiker life that I love and want and need (and fear) so much.

The fear I feel mostly comes down to questions I have about my own capacity for resilience. Who will I be when this hard thing I've chosen to do winds up feeling, well, hard? Have I overly romanticized a return to long-distance hiking over the past two years? Do I actually want to do this, or do I just *think* I want to do this? Am I even capable of hiking for almost 500 miles at high elevation? My limited previous experience above 10,000 feet was awful, and now I am going to try to spend an entire month up there in that low-oxygen world, walking almost non-stop all day every day? I shake my head once, twice, trying to physically clear out these fearful thoughts and questions. It's going to be what it's going to be, I remind myself. I am here, and all I can do is take the next step and then the next step and the next, and be open to whatever happens, trusting that I will handle it all as it comes.

I refocus my attention on Gent and Bugbite, the three of us walking side-by-side in a little line along the wide trail. It's a humid Sunday morning, everything damp and dripping from yesterday's torrential rainstorm. The sky is mostly clear today though, and I feel jittery with anticipation as we walk the first few miles in the thick, warm air, my heart thrumming like a kid on the first day at a new school. *This is actually happening!* After months of planning and spreadsheets and organizing my food and mailing all the resupply boxes, we have finally begun.

The route takes us along a mostly gravel path, well maintained with plenty of pit toilets and picnic tables. An hour goes by and I don't feel like I need a break yet but I take one anyway, first at three miles and then again at six miles, right before the trail winds away from Waterton Canyon. Take the breaks, I remind myself. Don't overdo it on day 1. There are so many more miles to go.

I think about this each time I answer curious questions from the many day hikers that pass us going the other direction, the folks who ask us excitedly if we're headed to Durango. Durango, the southern terminus of the Colorado Trail, 491 miles away.

"Hopefully!" I say to them. "That's the plan!"

To give any other answer seems ridiculous at this point, when we're only a few miles in. Am I going to Durango? I mean in theory, yes. But as someone who has already experienced what it feels like to quit a long-distance hike well before the planned end point, which I did on the Pacific Crest Trail in 2018 just after the halfway mark, I know that so much of this upcoming trek could be unpredictable. I might get sick; I might get hurt; I might need to deal with a family emergency; I might simply not want to hike anymore—all of that is possible. All of that and more.

But this is not the answer that most people want to hear. They want to hear that you are doing something big, that you are supremely confident you can go all the way.

"You've got to believe in yourself to get to Durango," one woman scolds me after I give her my honest (but apparently unsatisfactory) response of "maybe, hopefully!"

I nod and smile, continuing on without arguing, and yet I know for sure that she is wrong, that I do not have to believe in myself in order to get to Durango. I know this because in 2017, with laughably little experience, I set out to thru-hike all 800 miles of the rugged Arizona Trail. It took me 44 days to walk from Utah to Mexico, lonely and dehydrated beyond anything I had ever known, and it wasn't until early afternoon on day 41 that I first believed I could finish that hike. For 41 days I did not believe in myself, and yet I kept going anyway. Sometimes we don't need to believe in order to begin; sometimes the belief comes in the doing, built brick by brick along the way.

At the end of the canyon, six miles into our day, we veer off the wide path and onto a narrow ribbon of trail that climbs steeply up into the humid forest. Gent and Bugbite are in front of me—I am the slowest hiker in our group, the slowest hiker in pretty much every group I've ever been part of on a long-distance trek, and I prefer to be in the back so that I can go my own pace without feeling any pressure from folks behind me.

The trail is steep. I know that we are climbing, and that climbing is always tough, but right away I am surprised by how out of breath I feel, how quickly the sweat starts running down my chest and pooling in my bra. With all the frantic pre-trip preparations, wrapping up some work projects, saying goodbye to friends, driving from Oregon to Colorado, it's been weeks since I've gone on any kind of hike. And now, climbing up into this steamy forest above 5,000 feet my body is like, "um excuse me, what?"

It doesn't take long for me to fall behind the others, my menstrual cramps making me even slower than usual, and the effort of simultaneously bleeding and hiking drags my morale straight down. The trail keeps going up, just up up up, and I sweat through my socks and my shoes and all of my clothes. It feels shocking how acutely efforty this is, and I spend the next few miles thinking about how I want to talk to myself out here when things get hard. Working on that, on the way I speak to myself, is one of my main goals on this trek, building a more friendly relationship with myself, especially in moments when I feel frustrated by what I perceive to be my own weaknesses and inadequacies.

So I decide to try being my own cheerleader right now, even though it feels silly and forced.

You are doing such a good job sweating! I tell myself. *Look at you, regulating that body temp like a champ!*

This feels like an absurd compliment to give oneself, and it makes me laugh. And laughing lightens my mood, allows some of my fear (the fear that I'll spend the next month desperately trying to keep up with the others, always frantic, always behind) to dissipate.

I do not need to be afraid of that. Who cares if other people are faster than me? Who cares that long-distance hiking is hard? I love that it's hard. I am out here because it is hard, because it is an unparalleled privilege to be able to choose your suffering.

Eventually I catch up to the others, right before we stop for water at a small, fast-flowing creek where we learn that Bugbite's water filter is not working. This is not ideal—the first water stop and already a gear mal-function—but at least Gent and I both have filters we can lend them until one of the next town stops when they will be able to buy a new one.

I filter my own water and then I sit in the dirt, in a spot that's shaded by a towering tree, eating fruit snacks and Cheez-Its, drinking cold creek water, and this simple act ushers in a deep and immediate feeling of contentment. I didn't realize just how much I truly missed this, having all of my items on my back, exert-ing myself for hours and hours until I can finally just sit and rest and eat delicious things, letting the sweat dry all over my skin. Simple, peaceful, free.

I pack up when I'm done, putting the snacks back in my food bag, taking a swig of water and swallowing my next dose of Diamox. I have never taken this medication before, but it's supposed to help with high altitude acclimation. I started it a few days ago per my doctor's suggestion, to help ease the transition to climbing up into these mountains over the next few days, and as I put the little bag of pills away in my fanny pack I wonder if they will actually help me.

From there the afternoon is one tampon after another, hours of sticky sweat, a noticeable loss of appetite, and nausea that I assume is related to my period. The trail keeps us in the woods for hours, surrounded by big, leafy, overgrown plants that I gently move to the side with my hands as I hike through. We take another break all together at the top of the next big climb, where Bugbite and Gent eat more snacks and I slowly sip my water, trying to quell the continued nausea. I usually feel nauseated on the first day of my period, I remind myself. This is normal, it will pass. From there it's a four mile descent, down to the banks of the South Platte River, which we reach by 3:45pm.

"Do you want to camp here?" Gent asks.

I look around. It's a trailhead, so there are a handful of families nearby, kids playing in the water, a bunch of tents already pitched on the grass.

"Not really," I say. "It's kind of crowded, might be loud tonight. And we'd definitely be covered in condensation come morning."

Nicole Antoinette

The three of us huddle together and look at the map, trying to decide where to aim for instead. It looks like there's a flat enough spot about a mile away, up some steep switchbacks, and we agree on that.

"But let's stay here for a while," Bugbite says. "Eat an early dinner, rest."

So we do, pulling out our cold-soaking jars and adding water to our various mixtures of beans and rice. I have been going stoveless on hikes for years now, and so these dehydrated refried beans and I are in quite the committed relationship. But in this moment, with my nausea, the thought of eating even one bite of the cold-soaked beans I usually love makes me want to gag. I poke at them with my spoon, slowly chewing a few greasy tortilla chips and coaxing myself to just try, to do my best. I need to eat, I can't just not eat. It takes me the better part of an unpleasant hour though, to get it all down.

In that hour other hikers come and go, and our scattered conversations reveal that for most folks out here this is their first long hike. I think about this as we load up on water for both tonight and for tomorrow morning's 13-mile dry stretch, about the fact that I am not a beginner anymore. I didn't get into backpacking until I was in my early 30s, and prior to my first long hike I had only been car camping once (for one night) and backpacking once (for two nights), all in the few weeks right before setting out. Having so little experience made me feel like such an imposter on that first hike, and that initial imposter syndrome has proven difficult to overcome. But the truth is that I am not a beginner anymore. I still have so much to learn (there is always more to learn), but of all the hikers we have talked with throughout the day I am shocked when I realize that I am the most experienced one.

The final mile up to camp is steep, and the ground when we get there is too hard for me to get a proper tent pitch with my lightweight stakes, but I don't care. The joy I feel as I unfurl my quilt-style sleeping bag, climbing inside of it after this first 17.5 mile day and eating a small chocolate bar while the sun begins to set, that feeling is exactly why I'm out here. It's what I've been missing and craving and needing all along.

◁ ▷

Day 2

When I wake up everything is wet with condensation, and there's a small red fox staring at me through the mesh of my tent. I stay very still, staring back, watching until it darts away. I'm slow to get moving this morning, despite the anticipation of starting my first full day on the Colorado Trail. Sleep eluded me last night, between the awkward tent pitch and the adjustment process of trying to turn the outdoors into one's bedroom, but I didn't expect to sleep well on the first night so I find that I am not at all upset by it. Expectations, it seems, are everything.

I stuff my quilt away, down into the very bottom of my pack, careful in the process not to brush it against the wet walls of the tent. I can't imagine what the condensation would have been like had we camped down on the river bank, not when it's this wet all the way up here. We definitely made the right choice last night, hiking one more mile.

It's 6:45am by the time I hike out. Bugbite has gone off ahead, and Gent is only just starting to pack up. Our group's plan is to hike alone for most of each day, coming back together at lunch, at various break spots, and to set up camp. This is quite different from how Gent and I have approached previous trips—typically we hike together almost all day every day. And while it's fun to have company, especially during sections of trail that are challenging to navigate, he and I have come to realize that there is indeed such a thing as too much togetherness. For me it comes down to the fact that long-distance hiking often feels hard or boring (or both), and when I am with someone else during those times I easily fall into a pattern of complaining. When I am alone though, when there is no one to complain to, I simply get on with it. I hike. I rearrange my mindset and tap into that quiet, resilient place inside of me that thrives on seeing what is possible when things feel hard. Gent is like this too, in his own way, and so we have decided to use the Colorado Trail as a chance to experiment with a new kind of long-distance hiking together, one where we almost pretend we are each on our own solo trips, side-by-side. Plenty of hours of alone time, interspersed with the laughter and love and support that comes from having a trail family at camp and during breaks. The perfect compromise, or so we hope.

The trail climbs uphill right away as I leave camp, and I hike alone into the softest early rays of morning sun. I still feel nauseated, now with a new added tingling sensation in my hands that I've never felt before. I squeeze my fingers into tight fists as they go numb, almost as if these are not my hands at all, as if someone has stolen my regular hands and stitched ghost hands onto the ends of my forearms instead. What the hell, I think, struggling to properly grip my trekking poles with almost no sensation in my fingers. What is even happening right now.

This continues for about 45 minutes, ghost hands, nausea, a few desperate moments where it is too exposed in every direction for me to find the privacy to poop. Eventually I find a spot, tucked away in some trees to the left of the trail, and the experience of using my small shovel to dig a cathole while not being able to feel my hands is bizarre. Soon after I poop I feel better though, the tingling fades as quickly and inexplicably as it began, and I hike on into the warming sun.

Oh god, have you ever hiked all alone in the quiet morning hours as the world wakes up? I feel so lucky to be here right now that I almost start to cry.

At the top of the climb I sit for a while, eating the cold-soaked oatmeal into which I've mixed a little bag of nuts, chocolate chips, and dried fruit. It's good, a bit easier to stomach than dinner last night, and I begin to hope that whatever was going on with my appetite yesterday has passed.

Gent crests the hill just as I'm putting my things away, coming over to stop for his own break, and I try to describe my earlier ghost hands.

"Maybe you just slept weird?" he says. Yeah, maybe.

Before leaving I dig out my headphones, plug them into my phone, and put one in my right ear. I made myself an upbeat playlist last week, one that's titled HIKE HIKE HIKE, and as the trail flattens out I use the beat to cruise along at a quick pace. Through the trees, into an exposed meadow where tall grass waves gently in the breeze, views of the surrounding hills made more visible with every twist and bend of the trail.

After a while I hike into a more developed area, close to paved roads where I see cars and cyclists and other people going about their Monday morning business, and yet I feel detached from them, acutely aware that my whole existence is now this trail. I come to a junction and look across the road—where is the next trail badge for me to follow? I spot it, move in that direction, feet going from dirt to pavement to dirt again. It is only day 2 and this (walking from one trail badge to the next) is already all I am oriented toward. It surprises me how quickly one small symbol, the Colorado Trail badge, can become the focal point of my entire life; how quick I am to leave the rest of the world behind.

The terrain is drier on this side of the road, creek beds cracked and barren, and I stop to check both my map and my water report. I'm supposed to be meeting the others at a small stream for lunch, not too far from here, but it doesn't appear that any of the water sources in this area are still flowing. I take my pack off, eat a handful of fruit snacks, think about my almost empty water bottles. Hmm.

I keep hiking (what else am I going to do?) and by noon I've covered 12 miles. There is indeed a small stream where the map told me there would be, but Bugbite, who has been out in front of me all day, is not here. I sit down anyway, tired and thirsty, and wait for Gent. He must have been just behind me all morning because he arrives in under five minutes, but without knowing where Bugbite is we are at a loss for what to do next. Bugbite's water filter isn't working, so we know they'll need to borrow one of ours to fill up their bottles, so why aren't they here?

"Let's eat lunch and get water and then we'll keep going, try to find them," I say.

Gent agrees. We pull out our little butt pads, lay them on the ground, sit cross-legged facing each other and root around in our respective food bags. My nausea is back, completely eclipsing my appetite, and the thought of eating the ramen noodles with peanut sauce that I've been cold-soaking in my little jar all morning makes my stomach do a vicious flip-flop. This has never happened to me before, this kind of food aversion, neither on trail nor back at home, and as I sit and force the noodles into my mouth I fret about what it might mean. Is something actually wrong with me? How am I going to hike hundreds and hundreds of miles if every meal and snack feels like such a massive struggle? What if I can't eat enough? If I can't eat, I can't hike. I prod the unappealing noodles with my spoon, frowning.

After lunch Gent and I decide to hike together until we find Bugbite. It doesn't take long—just a little farther down the trail, at the next stream, a stream with much better flow than the shallow, dirty stream we stopped at. Bugbite is sitting in the dirt, eating snacks and tending to their thigh chafe, which looks red and irritated.

"This is probably not great," Bugbite says, looking down at the chafe.

"I have an inflamed ingrown scrotum hair," Gent says. We stare at him, grimacing.

"Well *my* swimsuit region is fine," I say, assessing my own body. "Other than the bleeding and cramping. But this morning I had ghost hands and all my food makes me want to die, so."

We are doing great.

The miles after lunch come slowly for me, much more slowly than they did this morning, almost as if I am crawling along the dusty trail, and it doesn't take long before I fall behind the others. Part of my languishing pace is that I am hot and uncomfortable, but part of it is my bladder—I cannot seem to stop peeing. Every half mile, sometimes every quarter mile, I am stopped on the side of the trail, grabbing for my pee rag, only just managing to get my shorts pulled down in time. Is this a menstrual thing? A side effect of the Diamox? What is even going on with my body today.

I find the others in the early afternoon, stopped for a break at Tramway Creek. This spot is about three miles from where we are planning to camp tonight, and it's still relatively early, so we decide to stay for a good long break, laying on the ground with our legs up a tree. This feels rejuvenating, the blood flowing away from my sore and swollen feet, and by the time we decide to start packing up I feel much better.

There are two other people at the creek with us now, friends in their 30s named Sean and Nick who came out here together and are both carrying enormous black backpacks. My pack is the smallest one I have seen on this trail so far, which is not an accident. I have found on my previous hikes that my enjoyment of the experience (as well as my ability to do it, physically) is largely related to how heavy my pack is. The heavier the pack, the more I struggle, and I am using the Colorado Trail as a chance to try a super lightweight frameless pack for the first time, filled with a pared down selection of gear.

"Okay, that looks like a child's pack," Nick says as I stand up from the dirt and put it on. "How can you possibly have everything you need in there?"

I shrug, not quite sure how to answer this. "It took me five years of hiking and a bunch of money invested into lightweight gear to get my pack this small," I say honestly. "And I'm resupplying more often, like every three or four days, so I don't have to carry as much food at one time, which helps."

I hike out behind Gent and Bugbite, and we move together down the trail for the remaining miles into camp. It's early when we get there, only 4:30pm, and at first it's tempting to keep going. There is still so much daylight left! But overdoing it this early into the hike would be stupid, when what our bodies need is to ease in. This is an endurance trek, a month-long adventure, and so much of the success with a goal like this comes down to knowing when to push and when to hold back. Right now we need to hold back.

So we take our time getting our respective tents set up, letting the late afternoon breeze dry last night's condensation away. I walk down to the roaring creek, where I unbutton my shirt, use a bandana to rinse the sweat from my face and body, comb my hair, and then sit on the ground to filter all the water I'll need for tonight and tomorrow morning. By the time I'm back at my tent I feel like a new person—clean, well hydrated, completely relaxed. I stretch for a while, eat my beans and rice, chat with the others until rain drops begin to fall and we all scurry into our tents, conversation fading away. I take some time to look at the map for tomorrow, and as I do I give myself a pep talk about what's coming.

Because what's coming is this: an 11-mile climb straight out of camp, plus another 8 miles of mostly climbing in the afternoon, taking us up to an elevation of 10,918 feet. I have not been above 10,000 feet since I was on the PCT in 2018, and I clearly remember how every single moment at that elevation felt absolutely miserable for me. I stare at the map, willing it to change, to say something else, to reveal an easier way, but no. The trail is the trail is the trail, and I must hike it exactly as it is.

Can I do this? I wonder. I *can* do this, right?

Well, maybe. I can maybe do this. But I decide that maybe is enough for now.

◁ ▷

Day 3

I pack up my tent quickly, all business, ready to try the "fake it til you make it" approach for today's daunting elevation gain.

I had some trouble falling asleep last night, the tat-tat-tat of light rain keeping me awake for hours, but it died down around midnight and I slept well from then on. So not a full night of rest, but better than nothing, and what I'm lacking in sleep I make up for in determination. I am determined to hike these miles today. Hike hike hike!

But first, oh god, I need to shit. The urge hits me like a battering ram a few minutes after I've left camp, and with the creek on one side of the trail and a steep upward slope on the other side there is absolutely nowhere good for me to go. But my body does not care about the inconvenient landscape, my body wants to shit *right now*. So I scramble up the steep slope, hand-over-hand in some spots, pack on my back, aiming for a large boulder that might be wide enough for me to duck behind. I wind up just barely making it there in time, narrowly avoiding shitting myself. Long-distance hiking: always finding ways to keep me humble.

Back on trail, hands sanitized, dirty toilet paper stashed in my trash bag, I begin to climb. I'm alone, with 4.3 miles until the top, and for the first few minutes I feel nothing but resistance. Resistance to the fact that this is hard, resistance to needing to do it at all. And it's funny, right, because I don't actually need to do this. I have chosen to do this. But choosing to do something doesn't mean that we don't sometimes suffer in the moment, and on this climb I quickly find myself falling down a mental spiral of "oh no, so hard, oh no oh no."

"Stop," I say to myself out loud, about a mile into the climb. I wrench my thoughts out of the spiral, gently label them as exactly what they are: thoughts, not facts. Name five things you can see right now, I prompt myself, hoping that this will keep me in the present moment, will help me to remember that this hike is not simply a physical challenge for me to "get through" but is instead an immersive nature experience that I want more than anything else.

"Small rocks on the trail underfoot," I say quietly, allowing myself to really take in the sight of them.

"Green, leafy trees," I say, a bit louder. I am all alone right now, why can't I be loud while I speak to the woods around me?

"Damp dirt from last night's rain! Fallen logs! Squishy moss!"

Five things, and I instantly feel better. Just by naming five things, I am here.

The rest of the climb passes quickly, engrossed as I now am in the world around me, in things other than how it feels to be in my body when conditions are hard. I stop at a dirt road crossing for a break, lean my pack up against the trail sign, settle down to eat some oatmeal. Gent catches me a few bites in and we take our break together, feeling good.

"I'm going to hike out alone from here," I say. "Does that feel okay for you?"

I tack the question on at the end, feeling guilty for wanting to be alone even though hiking alone for most of the day was our joint, shared plan. I care about his feelings of course, and yet I also wish that I wasn't so conditioned to first check in on other people's wants and needs before being really honest about my own. I want to hike alone right now, why can't I just say that? Why do I still feel like I need to ask everyone around me for permission?

I put one of my headphones in as I walk away, pumping myself up for the two and a half miles of climbing ahead. Soon I'm at 8,000 feet, then 8,200 feet, then 8,500 feet. The trail is rocky and I hike it. It's steep and I hike it. It's muddy and slippery and just up up up and I hike it, stopping twice to catch my breath. Eventually the endorphins kick in, that familiar rushing flood of "oh my god I am *doing this,*" and by the time I find Bugbite at a cold stream in the sumptuous damp woods of the Lost Creek Wilderness I feel euphoric.

The aspen trees are dense in all directions, their green leaves sparkling from the recent rain. Everything around us is bright, mist-soaked, alive. I see all manner of mushrooms—white ones and red ones and orange ones, big brown mushrooms the size of dinner plates—popping out across the forest as I filter my water and eat my packet of fruit snacks, my heart filled with a feeling of wonder and awe.

Gent catches up to us and gets his own water, and as I sit in the dirt with my friends I start to feel the encroaching numbness of yesterday's strange ghost hands sensation, except now the feeling is in my feet as well.

"What is happening to me," I say. "How am I going to hike if I can't feel my feet?"

"Maybe it's the elevation?" Gent says.

"Or the Diamox?" Bugbite adds. "It has to be one of the two, right?"

"I guess??"

We finish our break and spend the next few miles hiking together, carrying almost no water. There is so much water on this trail! Not carrying water makes my pack so light! I can't really feel my hands and feet, but the abundance of aspen trees makes me almost forget about that. The intricate little markings all over each tree trunk! The pale bark and the bright green leaves! Everything sopping wet! I splash around along the muddy trail, feet still numb, totally delighted.

Two miles, another stream, stopping to drink more water, this time with an added electrolyte tablet. I pull out my cold-soaking jar and add the ramen noodles and peanut sauce, trying to be optimistic that when the time comes to eat lunch my body and its persistent nausea will cooperate. Who knows.

There's a bit of cell service here, and we all lose ourselves in our respective internet holes, scrolling in a gluttonous way like little LTE goblins. Nom nom Instagram nom nom. I pull myself away first, hiking out, but soon the others reach me and then pass me, our group splintering apart in the afternoon as the trail pitches steeply upward, Bugbite and Gent faster out in front and me plodding along in the back. The terrain is not messing around—I gasp in the thinning air, taking short breaks every 100 steps or so. Soon the trail turns sharply to the left, the grade getting even steeper, even more rocky, and there's a moment slightly after that where my vision goes dark at the edges. I stop, sit on a wet log, head between my knees, breathe.

I fall out of linear time after that. I have never not been climbing this rock-strewn mountain in the thin wispy nothing air and I will never not be climbing it, that is how I feel. The earth smells pungent, raw, water-logged. I am exhausted, panting, light-headed, moving so slowly it feels like I might be standing still.

I find Gent with half a mile to go until the top, and he is in the mood to chat. I listen for a while, carefully lifting one leg and then the other up and over each of the big rocks, struggling to respond to him through the effort of my exertion.

"Babe," I finally say, gasping, "I can either talk to you or I can get myself to the top of this climb, but I definitely cannot do both."

He laughs. But I am not joking. He watches my face, nods, turns around and continues on in silence.

The top will never come, I think. Never ever ever. But then, all of the sudden, it does. 10,300 feet! I collapse in the wet dirt and put on my rain jacket. I try half-heartedly to eat my noodles, but the nausea is roiling and I just can't. I can't. So I suck down some plain peanut butter instead, eat a few bites of a slightly stale tortilla, put the jar of noodles back in my pack. How worried should I be about this whole food aversion thing, I wonder? What am I going to do with these un-eaten noodles? But soon the rain comes down harder, and I begin to shiver as my bare legs get pelted with icy water drops, and this shivering makes the nausea recede into the background of my mind at least a little bit for now. I hike out.

The trail descends for a few miles and I pound down it in the rain, all the elevation that I worked so hard to gain throughout the entire morning lost in a frac-tion of the time. I stop to put my pack cover on, it's really raining now, and I follow the trail as it drops down into a wide meadow. There's a stream running through this meadow, water brown with tannins, and the forest seems to spread out to infinity on the other side. Bugbite catches up to me and we hike the trail as it goes parallel to the stream, spotting a moose out in the distance (the first one that I have ever seen!) followed by another moose and another moose, just a little farther on.

The rain is coming down harder now, and we scurry under a grove of trees on a sloped hillside to hide. We are still trying not to overdo the miles, so there is no need to hike in the pouring rain just to get to camp even earlier than we already will. So we sit, and we wait for Gent, and we poke around in our food bags looking for the most appealing snacks. I eat an entire bag of chocolate covered pretzels, pretzels that were supposed to last me for the whole rest of this section. I watch myself do it, knowing full well that I am screwing over Future Me who will want chocolate pretzels and yet not have chocolate pretzels, but oh well. Current Me beats Future Me, at least in this moment.

It takes about 40 minutes for the rain to slow, to become just a chilly drizzle, and the three of us dart out from under our tree to hike the remaining mile or so to camp. Nick and Sean catch us moments later—we've named them the Black Pack Patrol, on account of their giant black backpacks. Sean tells us that he is being plagued by blisters of an increasingly worrying size, and I stop to dig out my first aid kit and give him some of my Wu-Ru, a type of wool that helps prevent (and cushion) your blisters.

"Just stuff it between your blister and your sock," I say. "It'll help!"

As I'm putting the first aid kit back and reattaching the rain cover, both guys remark again about how small my pack is.

"Do you want to hold it?" I ask. "Do you want to feel how light it is?"

"*Do you want to feel how light it is,*" Gent mimics in a teasing voice. "I thought we weren't gonna be dicks on this trail."

By which he means: there can be a real bro-y culture within the ultralight backpacking community where people brag about how low their pack weight is and offer to give other hikers gear advice and pack shake-downs even when those people definitely didn't ask for (and do not want) outside opinions. Lightweight gear is inaccessible for many people for lots of reasons—it is expensive, not often size inclusive, not available at many in-person stores, etc.—and when I chose to go the lightweight route with my current gear setup for this trail Gent and I joked (but it wasn't really a joke) about *not* becoming elitist dickwads. And yet here I am, offering to let two strangers hold my pack because it is so light. Maybe not my proudest moment?

"What the hell!" Nick cries as he takes it from me. "This is actually ridiculous. At camp tonight, will you show me all of your gear?"

"Sure!" I say, glad to know that he is sincerely in-terested and that maybe in this instance I am being helpful more than I am being a dickwad.

It only takes another ten minutes to reach camp, a large flat area under some trees with plenty of room for all five of our tents—me, Gent, Bugbite, Nick, and Sean, each in our own little area with plenty of space around us. Perfect.

I lay down my polycro groundsheet, a thin piece of delicate plastic that I'm not convinced is actually worth it, and then I go about pitching my tent on top of it. I love this tent, love how light and compact it is, but in heavy rain it's not the best. All of my items need to be positioned *just so* on the bathtub floor that rests on top of the mesh bottom of the tent, otherwise everything will get soaked throughout the night. And still, if the angle of the tent pitch is off even a little bit, or if it's a particularly windy night, the rain will blow in sideways through the mesh and everything will wind up soaked anyway, no matter how carefully it is all arranged.

Shelters set up, pads inflated, sleeping bags unfurled so they fluff up for maximum warmth between now and bedtime, we all grab our dinners and congregate together in the middle of our little tent village. Gent, Bugbite, and I are sitting on our butt pads (little pieces of foam we've brought to keep us from sitting directly on the ground) but Sean has a chair, a full-on *chair*, and I give him a look like, "Uh, dude, maybe this is why your pack is so heavy?"

"His trail name is gonna be The Chairman," Nick says, laughing.

"The Chairman!" we all yell.

We talk and laugh and eat together, the hoods of our rain jackets pulled all the way up, and I am having so much fun that I try to pretend that I'm not cold and wet to the point where I am slowly losing feeling in my body. But soon my teeth begin to chatter, and then the rain picks up, chasing us all into our tents just before 6:30pm. It is so early! Too early to be all alone in my tent and too bright in the sky to even think about falling asleep. So I sit there, and I touch all my things, move them around, try to position them out of reach of the rain. It's frustrating though, water is already pooling up on my groundsheet, making the mesh of my tent more wet than if the water had been free to just soak directly into the dirt below.

"Screw this," I say, climbing out of the tent and carefully pulling the groundsheet out from underneath it, balling it up to throw out once I get to town. Screw this ridiculously useless piece of plastic, no more groundsheet for me.

Back in the tent I strip off my wet rain jacket, shove it in the corner where it can't drip on anything else, put on my puffy coat instead, zip it all the way up, hood pulled tight around my face. I take off my shoes (wet) and socks (wet), stack them in the corner with the rain jacket and put on my little lightweight down booties, which will help to keep my always-cold feet warm throughout the night. I then set about clipping my quilt to my sleeping pad. It's an ingenious system really, wherein a series of clips are sewn to the sides of the quilt and you attach those clips to sturdy pieces of cord that wrap around your sleeping pad, which then allows you to have the lightweight benefits of a quilt without the draftiness. I was on the fence about whether to bring my quilt on this trip though, versus my super warm proper sleeping bag. The quilt is rated for 22 degrees, which would usually be fine for an August hike, but way up here in the high mountains? I am not so sure. Especially since I know from experience that as such a cold sleeper I am really only comfortable about 20 degrees above the temperature rating of a sleeping bag—meaning that this quilt would be great for me in the low 40s, but no colder. My big floof sleeping bag on the other hand, a true mummy bag rated for 10 degrees, has kept me cozy in temps down to the high 20s, but of course it's much larger and heavier, which is why I didn't bring it. Maybe that was a mistake?

I lay there for a while thinking about this, wiggling around in my quilt wearing all of my clothes, trying to get warm. Worrying about whether or not you will be warm is not going to make you any warmer, I remind myself. So instead I begin to list out all the animals I've seen on the first three days of this hike—lots of bunnies and deer, one snake, one fox, three moose, a small herd of mountain goats, eleventy thousand chipmunks and squirrels. I wonder what each of these creatures is doing right at this exact moment. Are they hiding from the rain? Are they totally unfazed? How can I become unfazed, too?

Eventually the sun falls away over the horizon and darkness settles in around me. I am awake long into the night, listening to the sound of water pouring down against the walls of my tent, not quite warm enough but loving that good heavy feeling in my legs that lets me know that I'm doing it, I'm out here—55 miles down, and it's all just one day at a time.

◁ ▷

Day 4

It rains all night, thick condensation gathering inside the tent that showers down on my face every single time I move. So basically it is raining both outside *and* inside the tent now. Ugh.

Nicole Antoinette

Bleary-eyed and exhausted as the sun comes up, I struggle to pack up all of my sopping wet things in the cold biting air with increasingly numb hands. It's just regular numb though, not ghost hands, so that feels like a win.

Pack on the ground by my feet, I curl my fingers in front of my mouth, blowing warm air on them to try and give myself enough dexterity to zip up my rain jacket. It doesn't work though, so I hike out with the jacket on but flapping wide open, moving as fast as I can to try and warm up.

It's 16.6 miles to the highway from here, and our goal is to get there in time to hitch into the town of Fairplay before the post office closes this afternoon, to pick up our resupply boxes. This is doable, I tell myself, even though I was awake almost all night and I can feel the exhaustion like thick sludge throughout my body. But it's fine that I am tired. I can do this tired. I've done it so many times before.

So I hike and I hike, hands slowly warming up enough that I can finally zip my rain jacket, and then later I warm up enough that I don't need the jacket at all. The sky is clear, a soft blue directly above me with the haze of wildfire smoke way out in the distance. I stop mid-morning to poop and it feels... bad. Really bad. Wondering-if-I-somehow-drank-unfiltered-water bad.

Gent catches me as I get back on trail, dousing myself in hand sanitizer from the wrist down.

"I am having a *morning*," I tell him.

"I see that," he says. "Want to hike together for a while?"

So we do, covering two downhill miles on terrain that's gentle enough for us to talk, surrounded by wildflowers that are so abundant and beautiful that I forget about the hellish poop experience I just endured.

We catch up to Bugbite, stop together at a fast-flowing stream, stare at the mountains, sit in the sun, eat some snacks. All of the sudden I need to run off and dig another cathole, this time even more urgently than before, and the look on my face when I come back must be that of a car-crash survivor because Gent just goes, "That terrible, huh?"

"I'd rank it a 3 out of 10," I say. "If a 1 out of 10 is the kind of poop experience that's so bad you need to burn your shorts afterward and jump immediately into the shower, this was definitely a 3."

Like I said, I am having a *day*.

We all hike out together from there, but it takes less than a quarter mile for me to fall behind. I watch as my friends travel quickly up and over the top of the next climb, whereas I am back here at the bottom of the climb, feeling like I am moving in slow motion, like the combination of woes in my body (the not sleeping, the whatever is happening to my digestive system) is something that I cannot overcome.

I hike on, frustrated. This feeling, the feeling of being so depleted that it's as if even my breath and bones and blood are tired, is a feeling I am so familiar with from past long-distance hikes. It's the feeling of: Can't I just fucking lay down on the side of the trail and close my eyes for the rest of the day, for three days, for all the days, for eternity? I know this dramatic feeling all too well. I hate this feeling. This feeling is the thing I forget about when I have been off trail for a while, when I am well-rested and covered in blankets at home, laptop propped in front of me so I can look through my gorgeous hiking photos, anxious to get back out on trail as soon as I can. It's an all-encompassing feeling, one that never seems so bad when I think about it in retrospect. But in the moment? When I have barely slept for multiple nights in a row and I am pushing myself up a steep climb using the last remaining dregs of my own willpower, it feels awful. Everlasting. Unendurable. And when my friends are out ahead of me somewhere, when I am alone in the back of the pack, my mind is quick to make up all kinds of stories about how everyone else is better at this than me and so what am I even doing, thinking I will be able to keep up with them?

I stop for more water with 6 miles to go until Kenosha Pass, which is where the trail will cross the highway that leads into town. As I alternate between filtering water directly into my mouth and eating handfuls of Cheez-Its, I give myself a little pep talk. I remind myself that I am out here to practice self-kindness. That how I talk to myself in moments when I perceive that I am bad at something, when I am stuck in a loop of comparing myself to others, when things feel hard— that is the work. I want to be so gentle to myself, so encouraging, not making it "mean" anything that I am always the slowest one, and today is the perfect opportunity to practice that.

So I put my snacks away, I hike out, and I try it. I try to say kind things to myself. I try to become okay with the fear I feel, the fear that my friends will have been waiting for me at the highway for so long, that they will be annoyed, that I will be holding them back.

This internal rearranging sort of works, a little bit at least, but still I do not let myself stop for any more breaks. I want to stop multiple times, both because I am so tired and because the mountain views are spectacular, but what if I take a break and fall even further behind?

So I don't take breaks, and I don't eat enough or drink enough, and by the time I reach the trailhead I am angry. Angry at myself, mostly, but also irrationally angry at my friends. Why do they have to be so god-damn fast? In this moment it feels like they are fast *at* me, and it fills me with rage.

"Hey!" Gent and Bugbite call out from their little spot in the shade, oblivious to my inner turmoil.

"How long have you been here?" I demand, dropping my pack and grabbing whatever snacks I can reach to start quelling the low blood sugar I didn't attend to at all over the past three hours.

"Um, maybe 10 minutes?" Gent says. "15 at the most."

10 minutes? *Only 10 minutes*? I hiked myself into the ground all afternoon, thinking they were so far ahead of me, and they have only been here for TEN MINUTES? I put my head in my hands, take some deep breaths, feel like maybe I am going to cry.

I eat some chips, drink electrolyte water, gather myself emotionally. It only takes a few minutes after that to hitch a ride from a man in a pickup truck, who drops us at the gas station on the outskirts of town. It's about a mile walk from there to the post office, and after the post office we collapse at a table outside the local restaurant. Are we heading back to the trail after this? Or are we gonna get a motel room instead.

I eat a BLT and a basket of crispy tater tots, drink three large glasses of ice water, begin to feel like a human again. There's a motel right by the highway and we get a cheap room, one that doesn't have a fan or any kind of air circulation but does have a big fly strip hanging from the ceiling with a swarm of dead flies covering almost every inch of it. But what do I care about dead flies when there is a hot shower and ice cream from the nearby Dollar Store and the chance to sleep in an actual bed? If dead flies hovering above my head all night is the price of admission for those other things, I will gladly pay it.

So we shower, eat whatever we can reach while being horizontal, zone out, scroll around the internet on our phones, turn the lights off at 9pm. The relief I feel as I lay there in the dark, with zero condensation dripping on my face, is immediate and profound. I smile to myself, a huge and genuine grin, and then, barely a few moments later, I am deeply asleep.

◁ ▷

Day 5

Motel sleep is the best sleep and I wake up feeling like I can do anything. Anything!

The irony of not sleeping well for days and days is that the elation I then experience once I finally *do* sleep is so exquisite that it almost makes the prior agony of sleep deprivation feel worth it, just for the bliss of that one morning when I explode out of bed like, "HELLO WORLD, I AM ALIIIIIVE!"

That is me today, obnoxiously grateful for the simplest pleasures of embodiment.

So my morale is sky high as I set out to do my laundry, wearing only my puffy jacket and the sheer tights that I sleep in, which are the only items of clothing that I am willing to not wash right now. Everything else though? Everything else is filthy.

I insert the quarters and start the washing machine before heading over to the nearby coffee shop, where I order a large earl grey tea and a bagel with cream cheese. I wait for the alarm on my phone to go off, telling me it's time to move the clothes into the dryer, and in the meantime I eat, get a refill on my tea, wait some more. I love this feeling though, love not feeling rushed, love that I'm so well-rested, love that for once in my hiking life I do not dread the idea of leaving town to get back on trail.

This is something I typically struggle with, the allure of town comforts combined with the feeling of fear and imposter syndrome I used to experience whenever it was time to load my pack up and head back into the woods. It's hard to explain, but on all of my past hikes, even when things were going well, I have been plagued by a constant undercurrent of doubt, a core questioning of whether or not I would be able to do what I set out to do. And so whenever I'd make it through a section of trail and get into town I'd feel like, "oh thank god that wasn't the section where everything imploded on me," but then the closer I'd get to leaving town the more fearful I'd become that the *next* section would definitely be the one where everything imploded. I didn't trust myself to be able to make it any farther, not when whatever miles I had somehow already accrued felt to my doubting mind like a total fluke, and so I came to dread the moment when I had to leave town, convinced that I wouldn't make it through whatever waited for me in the section ahead.

But right now I do not feel any of that fear or doubt. I feel completely ready to leave town, even excited to get back to hiking, and this is so unprecedented, so unfamiliar, that it makes me laugh with surprise in the middle of the aisle at the grocery store later that morning. I cannot wait to keep hiking! Who knew?!

I push my small cart up and down all the aisles, carefully selecting the items I most want as a supplement to what was in the resupply box I picked up from the post office yesterday. All of my main meals and snacks were in that box, but I want to try packing out more fresh food from each town on this trip, and so I leave with a bagged salad, a small thing of hummus and pretzels, a pound of sweet ripe strawberries, and a family size bag of white cheddar popcorn that I grabbed at the last minute and have no idea how to fit inside my pack.

Back in the hotel room I play an intense game of gear Tetris, trying to squeeze everything in, eventually realizing that as long as I strap the popcorn to the top of my pack I can make it work. Okay, excellent, let's do this.

Gent, Bugbite, and I walk down to the busy intersection, thumbs out, trying to hitch a ride. Cars fly past us for about ten minutes, the drivers neither slowing down nor making eye contact with us, and I start to feel discouraged. Is anyone going to pick us up? Should we move somewhere else? Is there a better spot to hitch from if we head down the road?

Hitchhiking makes me feel so vulnerable, entirely at the whims of random strangers, and I am comforted that at least I'm not doing this alone right now. Hitching by myself (while definitely easier, because people do tend to stop more often for a solo woman hiker) feels fraught with much more uncertainty and risk.

But wait! An old, blue, beat up van is pulling over just ahead. We huddle together at the passenger door, peer inside as the window comes down.

"You're welcome to squeeze in, if you can!" the driver says. He's young (early 20s maybe?) and tells us he's driving out to Martha's Vineyard for a wedding. There's a bed in the back of his van, and the entire floor space between the bed and the front seats is covered with luggage and instruments and amps, with all kinds of other miscellany and trash shoved into even the smallest open corners and crevices in between.

"Yeah okay," Gent says. "Thanks!"

He opens the passenger door and climbs in, as per our usual trail agreement in which Gent, the 6'1 white man, takes responsibility for making conversation with our (almost exclusively) white male hitchhike drivers, many of whom want to talk about motorcycles and cars and weed and "the state of this country" and "what's wrong with America" — topics that I personally have zero interest in delving into with strange men while trapped in their vehicles, thank you very much.

So Gent does it instead, for which I am grateful, and in the meantime Bugbite and I try to situate ourselves on the bed in the back of the van, our packs balancing precariously on this dude's many piles of stuff. There are no seatbelts back here, so we sit toward the edge of the bed, within easy reach of the side windows, prepared to use our arms to brace ourselves against the windows (and each other) if necessary. Getting to and from this town marks Bugbite's first hitching experience, and the look on their face as the van skids and lurches back into traffic and then picks up speed along the highway can best be described as: "Please don't tell my mom about this."

We bump along down the road, music blaring, Gent and the driver talking loudly enough in the front to make their voices carry over both the music and the wind that's whistling in through the open windows, while Bugbite and I sit silently and instead communicate with each other through various stages of widening our eyes.

There's one point when the van swerves into the shoulder of the road, narrowly avoiding the semi-truck ahead, and as I look down over the guardrail at the many hundreds (thousands?) of feet below the steep drop off on the other side I wonder what it is that I think I am doing. Do I believe that the laws of physics do not apply while hitchhiking? Do I think that being a long-distance hiker in need of a ride back to trail somehow creates a protective bubble around me and whichever dude's vehicle I climb inside of? Apparently yes, because here I am, no seatbelt, perched on the edge of a strange man's bed going 70 miles per hour.

At the trailhead (finally, safely) the guy pulls over, and he offers us a gulp of his "special home-brewed mushroom tea" on our way out.

"Uh, we're all set," we say. "But thanks for the ride!"

We grab our stuff, closing the doors and turning toward the trail as he drives away.

"Is that dude drinking some kind of liquid drug tea that he brewed *in his vehicle* while driving across the country?" I ask. "Is that who we just drove with for 20 miles?"

The others laugh and I do too, because now that we're safe it does feel kind of funny, just another part of this wild adventure. But underneath the laughter I'm hearing something else, some kind of warning bell in my head that reminds me that I can say "no" out here, that just because someone pulls over and offers me a ride doesn't mean I need to take it.

It's noon by the time we start hiking, all three of us moving down the trail in a single file line. Our plan is to go about 11 miles today and camp near the summit of Georgia Pass, which is where, according to a local friend, "the *real* beauty of this trail begins."

It's five miles of up and down and up and down from the trailhead at Kenosha Pass to the first water source, a small creek with a fast flow in the thick forest with warm sunlight and afternoon shadows filtering down through the many branches. I sit in the shade and eat the bagged salad I packed out from town, feeling smug about my leafy greens until I realize how hard it actually is to eat salad with a spoon. It's the only utensil I've got though, so I make it work, kind of dumping lettuce into my mouth a little at a time, spooning the croutons and dressing and cheese in after it.

I sit there for a half hour, chatting with the other hikers who come by, most of whom we met on day 1. They've been behind us, but they didn't go into Fairplay to resupply so our time in town allowed them to catch up. It's the accordion effect of long-distance hiking, wherein you see the same people over and over again but at such unpredictable times, depending on how many miles you're each hiking per day and who stops in which town and for how long. The Colorado Trail is the first big hike for all of these folks, and I listen as they get to know each other with talk of gear and blisters and "where are you from" and "what brought you out here" and "okay but how do I make my pack not feel so fucking heavy?"

They look at me as they say this, at my small pack, and I shrug. I do not feel like going into detail about my gear right now, not when my morale is so high and my hiking boner is this huge and all I want to do is keep moving. So I gather my trash, stuff it in the side pocket next to my water bottle, wave to everyone, and hike out, still riding that sweet sweet feeling of a good night's sleep and the resulting love affair that I seem to be having with hiking today.

Five more miles, all alone, to an ice cold creek that numbs my fingers as I sit in the dirt and filter a liter of water. I take a few sips, following the freezing sensation as it moves from my lips to my tongue to my throat on down, making me shiver. The sun is still up but the temperature is dropping, and I rub my hands against the goosebumps on my arms. There's a little more climbing still to go, to the summit of Georgia Pass, and I know that climbing will warm me up. So I slip the now full water bottle back in my pack, eat a few strawberries, and go. The strawberries are delicious, so much fresher and more flavorful than anything else

I usually eat on trail, but a pound of strawberries does indeed weigh a full pound, and I can feel the added heft of them on my back as I hike up into the quiet of the mountains.

I reach our planned camp spot at 5:15pm, body still singing with energy, realizing that my motivation has not flagged once all day. It's windy up here though, and I look around the exposed plateau just below the summit of Georgia Pass, feeling worried. There's no way this is a good place to camp, right? Not way up here with no tree cover, not with the potential storm clouds gathering in the distance.

Bugbite is already here, sitting on the grass, and Gent arrives a few minutes later, immediately dropping his pack with a dull thud and sitting down as well. No one says much—both of them are at the opposite end of the mood spectrum from me, deep in a low morale moment, ready to be done hiking for the day but agreeing that this spot is too exposed to be safe.

"Maybe try eating something?" I say. "Chocolate is good for low morale."

We look at our maps, scanning the five and half mile descent down to the Swan River, which it looks like we will need to reach because there isn't anywhere good to camp in between.

"Can you do another 5ish miles?" I ask them.

Bugbite nods. Because what is the alternative, really? We all know we aren't going to stay here.

"My head hurts," Gent says, offering no other answer to my question. It is probably the elevation, I feel it too. We're at 11,875 feet now, and this is the highest I have been in over three years, since the week I spent in the Sierra Nevada mountains right before I quit my attempted thru-hike of the Pacific Crest Trail.

"Want to take some ibuprofen?" I ask him, holding out the ziplock bag of pills I keep in my fanny pack.

"Yeah," he says. "My achilles hurts too. Thanks."

I wait while the others gather themselves, and then together we crest the summit of the windswept pass in the early evening light. We've got 5.4 miles to go now, down down down the other side of the pass, and it is during this descent that I find that I am absolutely fine until I'm not, until we're two miles from camp and my seemingly infinite morale takes an unexpected nosedive, many aches and pains announcing themselves loudly and all at once, including a sudden throbbing sensation in my left big toe that makes me nervous, makes me think about the time on a different long-distance hike a few years ago when Gent had to drill holes in both of my big toenails to pop the giant blisters that had formed underneath. Oh god, I think. Is that happening again? I hike slowly, falling behind the others, feeling scared.

You're fine, I try to tell myself. It's just a random bruise or something. You are not allowed to spiral out about this. No spiraling out!

I take a deep breath and slowly pick my way down the steep rocks toward the Swan River, thinking about how drastically one's mood can change during a single day in the backcountry. Our no-seatbelts-mushroom-tea-hitchhike feels like an eternity ago, as does my earlier excitement about hiking. Did all of that really happen today?

When I finally reach the flat ground near the river it's 7:15pm, the latest I have gotten to camp so far on this trip. I feel stressed about that, about wanting to get everything set up before dark, which compounds the stress I already feel about my pulsating toe. It's cold down here, the temperature continuing to drop, and I shiver as I spin around in circles a few times, trying to decide what to do first when it seems like all of my needs are screaming for attention at the exact same time.

Stop, I think. *Breathe.*

A few deep breaths later and I am slightly calmer, at least calm enough to go into what I call "triage mode", wherein many problems need to be solved efficiently and in quick succession and I am the one who has to do it all, and so I must get my shit together and do it calmly and systematically, one thing at a time.

First: drop the pack and lean it up against a tree. Great, no more heaviness on my shoulders. Next: put on my puffy jacket and zip it up, change into my wool tights. Okay, excellent, no more being cold. Then: scan the surrounding area, choose a flat enough spot for the tent, pitch the tent, unfurl the quilt, blow up the sleeping pad. There, that's done. Swallow some ibuprofen, poke at my toe, whimper, stretch, hope for the best.

The last thing on my triage list is to eat, but I do not want anything in my food bag. The salad was mostly fine earlier, as were the strawberries, but my ever-present nausea and its accompanying gut-churning sensation is making almost all food seem deeply unappealing. I've been trying not to dwell on this too much, hoping (pretending?) that it would go away on its own, but it does not seem to be going away. I am nauseated pretty much all of the time now, and in turn I am not eating enough, which has me worried.

You have to eat, I tell myself. *You cannot hike 500 miles if you don't eat!*

So I do, forcing down every bite of the beans and rice, gagging a few times. It takes almost an hour to get through it all but eventually I do, and I crawl into my tent feeling relieved. I did it: I solved all of my problems tonight.

I fall asleep quickly after that, lulled by the sounds of the nearby river. I get up to pee at 2am and when I do, oh my god, glittering stars are spilled all across the sky. I pull my tights down and squat in the dirt, peeing as I rest my elbows on my knees, sleepy eyes going wide at the light-show above me.

This is magic, I think. And yet somehow it is real.

◁ ▷

Day 6

By the time the first rays of color begin to splash across the sky I have already been awake for a few hours, curled up in my quilt, too cold to fall back asleep.

I know that we are camped near a river in a bit of a valley right now, which is likely a contributing factor, but the knowledge that I have so many more nights at even higher elevation to come has me concerned.

I definitely should have brought my warmer sleeping bag. And yet I didn't bring my warmer sleeping bag. My warmer sleeping bag is in my van, parked at a friend's house all the way back in Denver. So now what? I am already wearing all of my layers; there's nothing else I can do to stay warm.

Except hike. Right now I can get up and I can start hiking. Hiking will warm me up!

It's just past 7am by the time I leave camp, later than I expected but that's mostly because it took me so long to choke down my breakfast. It's two miles to water this morning, and it feels like it takes me an eternity to get there. My legs are super heavy from yesterday's climb up and over Georgia Pass in which I didn't take nearly enough breaks. I think maybe I'm dehydrated, too. And everything I try to eat tastes terrible, sour and chalky on my tongue. Is this still a side effect of altitude acclimation? Is it the Diamox? Shouldn't I be feeling better by now?

At the creek I sit on the edge of a wooden footbridge and filter a liter of water, water that's so cold that it makes my fingers ache as I hold and squeeze the filter bag. There are two other hikers here, friendly guys in their 20s who have set out together to complete their first thru-hike.

"George and Alex," they say, introducing themselves. "We don't have trail names yet."

Alex, it seems, is feeling good. George, however, is not. He picks at the edge of his knee brace, telling us the litany of ailments that have plagued him throughout this first section. Listening makes me nostalgic in a way, makes me think back to 2016 when I did my own first long hike—the 460-mile Oregon section of the PCT—before which I had almost zero backpacking experience. I was a total beginner, and throughout the first week on trail it honestly felt like a bomb had gone off inside my body. I remember sitting in the dirt on day 3, needle in hand, desperately trying to decide whether it was better to pop my throbbing blisters or leave them alone. Every single part of me hurt that day, my muscles and tendons and bones and skin and soul. Can one's eyelashes be sore? One's lips and fingernails? That is how I felt.

And so when George tells us that he's been having such a tough time in his body, my heart swells with empathy. Because I know that body pain also causes emotional pain, wherein you spend the entire hiking day thinking about whether or not you should quit, because quitting is the only thing that would stop the pain. But you don't want to quit! You've been looking forward to this adventure for so long! You've planned so much! Bought all the gear! Saved all the money! Taken the time off work! It's an agonizing conundrum.

"We're going into Breckenridge later today," George says. "To resupply."

"If you have the budget and the time to take a full rest day in town tomorrow you should absolutely do it," I say, breaking my own rule not to give unsolicited advice to other hikers.

"Yeah," George says, looking over at Alex sheepishly. "Maybe."

Oh, I realize. George is afraid that he's holding Alex back. This too feels deeply relatable to me—I have been the injured one, the slower one, the unhinged sleep deprived one, and that feeling of knowing exactly what you need to do to take care of yourself and yet feeling so guilty that what you need would cause other people to change their own plans to accommodate said needs in order to keep hiking with you is its own kind of pain.

"You're gonna be okay," I tell him, standing up and grabbing my pack. "Your only job is to make it to Breck today. Try not to worry about anything else."

I hike out, following the trail as it winds away from the creek, turning sharply upward, and for miles afterward that is all I do: I go up and up and up and up. It's not exceptionally steep, and so I am surprised by what a hard time I'm having. I stop every third of a mile or so, lean my forehead on my trekking poles, cough, steady my breathing, continue on.

Why is this so hard, I wonder. Why why why.

But I realize after a while that it is actually okay that it is hard, because I have spent the past ten years since getting sober strengthening my ability to hold the both/and of life where something can be hard *and* worth it; tough in the moment *and* nowhere else I'd rather be. I have long understood that type II fun—the kinds of experiences that are maybe not so fun in the moment but very fun in retrospect—is in my blood, and I am so grateful to be having that kind of fun right now.

So I keep going up, knowing that eventually the top will come, and it does. It feels anti-climactic though, no summit, no views, just a flatter version of the same trees and dirt. Gent and Bugbite are already here, sitting on their butt pads just off to the side of the trail. I join them, laying out my own pad and taking my cold-soaking jar out from the mesh pocket in the front of my pack. Inside the jar is my oatmeal, all re-hydrated and ready to go, but the extent to which I do not want to eat this oatmeal (or anything else) is astounding. I just climbed uphill for so long, shouldn't I be hungry? At this exact moment I have over 3,600 miles of long-distance hiking experience, and never once in all those miles have I felt anything close to this kind of food aversion.

I open the screw top lid on the jar, poke at the oatmeal with my spoon, hesitating. It's filled with everything I like: toasted pecans and chocolate chips, coconut milk powder and dried cranberries, and yet even the smell of it seems to turn my stomach. I eat a few bites, take sips of electrolyte water in between, take a few more bites. Eating is typically one of the best parts of a long-distance hike, but in this moment it feels like its own kind of endurance challenge and I hate it. I just absolutely hate it.

I spend about 45 minutes sitting there like that, talking to other hikers as they pass, trudging through my oatmeal. Bugbite packs up and leaves, and soon I do too, with Gent following behind me. We've got a big descent ahead, the cruel and immediate loss of all that elevation we just worked so hard to gain. Down and down we go, and if the climb felt hard it is nothing compared to the descent. What is going on with me today? It's as if my body has forgotten how to hike, as if placing one foot in front of the other is a puzzle I am no longer able to solve.

I descend and descend, and the constant downward motion wrecks my legs. An hour goes by, and I am moving so slowly now that I cannot believe Gent hasn't asked to pass me yet.

"Are you *sure* you don't want to go ahead?" I ask for the twelfth time.

"I'm sure," he says. "I like hiking with you."

"My legs feels like they've been pumped full of lactic acid," I say. "As if you could prick them with a pin and lactic acid would just gush right out."

Lactose acid, Gent starts calling it. "What if your legs were actually filled with lactose acid?"

Soon afterward the idea of having lactose acid in my legs somehow morphs into me having what Gent decides are now called *spoiled milk legs*. It makes sense really, because that is indeed how I feel.

So I hike downhill on my spoiled milk legs, taking little mincing steps on this section of trail that has been deeply rutted out by mountain bikes. It's impossible to take normal steps here, to keep any kind of consistent stride, and by the time we reach a wooden bench on a small flat area overlooking the mountains beyond it feels like I am more ready to sit down than I have ever been in my entire life.

We sit there together, Gent and I, his arm around my shoulders and my head tipped to the side to rest on his chest. We eat Cheez-Its and fruit snacks and nuts, and I swallow some ibuprofen with what's left of my water. I didn't expect these miles to take anywhere near this long, which means that I have run out of water sooner than I expected and therefore have the beginnings of a dehydration headache. There's supposed to be a small water source in a few miles though, so I drag myself back to standing, all the while keeping up an internal monologue of "you can do it, you're fine, you can do it, you're fine."

And while I might not actually be fine it is in fact true that I can still do it, hiking one step at a time until I reach Horseshoe Gulch and the small pile of stones that someone has shaped into the number 100. 100 miles! We have now hiked 100 miles.

Bugbite is here (and has been here for at least an hour already, apparently not suffering from spoiled milk legs), as are George and Alex and a few other hikers.

"100 miles!" I call out as I get closer to them.

"100 miles!!" everyone says back.

There's water flowing down in the small stream, but it's shallow and hard to gather, and I'm too tired to finagle a better collection method. Plus it has just started raining, and so I take what little water I've managed to get and dash over to a nearby tree, shoving all my items further under its low branches in hopes of staying dry.

Conversation flows all around me, laughter and gear talk and the making of various plans for what every-one is going to eat once they get to Breckenridge, but my friends and I are not stopping in Breckenridge and this makes me feel as though I am not really a part of this group, as if they are doing their own thing and I am just somehow also here. So I zone out, sip some water, eat a few handfuls of whatever I can most easi-ly reach from my food bag, knowing I should be eating and drinking way more than I am, knowing this will come back to haunt me later today but for some rea-son that knowledge does nothing to make me actually take better care of myself in the moment.

The rain stops as suddenly as it started, and even though everyone is still talking and laughing I feel an inexplicable urge to flee. I stuff all of my things away, back into my pack, and abruptly stand up.

"Okay bye!" I say, acutely aware of how awkward I'm being.

"Wait," Alex says. "We'll come with you!"

He and George gather their things as well, and together we form a single file line headed uphill away from the stream. I'm in front, which immediately makes me feel anxious. Am I going fast enough? Do they wish they were in front instead? Is this pace okay?

"Do you guys want to pass me?" I ask. "You can set the pace if you want."

They shake their heads, smiling, seemingly happy to tuck in behind me and ask me a barrage of questions as they follow my clacking trekking poles up and down the trail. I didn't want them to join me at first, wanted to be alone with my weird mood and my spoiled milk legs, but having new people to talk to makes the hiking feel easier and soon we've gone just over three miles and are descending down to a small pond that our map lists as a water source even though it's apparently right in the middle of a residential area, expensive vacation homes surrounding it on all sides. It's disorienting how quickly we went from the quiet wooded trail to this developed community on the outskirts of Breckenridge, and I feel painfully self-conscious as I drop my pack and scramble down to the pond to gather a few liters of water. Is this really okay? I feel filthy. Is someone about to walk onto their million dollar front porch and yell at me for disturbing their pristine pond?

I collect my water as quickly as I can, scurrying over to join Bugbite who is sitting in a semi-hidden spot underneath a tree.

"Are we even allowed to be here?" I ask.

Bugbite shrugs. Earlier today, just going off what we could see on our map, we thought we might be able to camp near this pond, but there is no way. The highway is on one side of us and the fancy homes are on the other—definitely not a place for dirty hikers to spend the night. So we sit quietly, a little stressed about where to go, waiting for Gent who definitely should have been here by now. How bad is his achilles pain, I wonder, to be slowing him down this much?

My worry intensifies once I see him descending down the trail toward us, the unnatural movement of his gait like a glaring neon sign that screams "I AM IN PAIN!!"

"Shit," I whisper. Shit shit.

He joins us, misery etched into his face as he too sits cross-legged on his butt pad underneath the branches of the tree.

"Not good?" I say.

"Not. Good." he responds.

We all sit there like that for a while, tucked under the tree to wait out another sudden burst of rain, each lost in our own inner worlds. I am not sure what Bugbite and Gent are thinking as we sit here, but I know that I am thinking about how badly I want to be done hiking for the day. We haven't even covered that many miles, 15 maybe? But I am exhausted. And worrying about Gent is more exhausting still. Is he going to be okay? What can I do to help him? Will he even be honest with us about his true pain level, about what is going on in his achilles tendon? How soon can we find a secluded spot to pitch our tents for the night so that he can be done?

"I don't know where we're going to camp," I say, looking at the upcoming stretch of trail on my map. We'll cross a few major roads soon, the ones that lead into town, but then after that it's a single track path that climbs up for nine straight miles with few water sources and even fewer flat spots for sleeping. *Not good* indeed. Especially not when I know that uphill terrain is the worst for Gent's achilles, but what else are we going to do? We definitely can't stay here.

"Let's cross the roads and just start the climb," I say, forcing much more optimism and cheerfulness into my voice than I actually feel. "I bet we'll find a stealthy little spot to camp in no time!"

The others look at me skeptically, but I fix the most genuine-seeming smile possible on my face and try to will them both to believe that it will be okay. Bugbite acquiesces first, getting up to hike out with me, Gent saying that he'll follow behind once he's gotten a little more rest.

My pack is heavy as we get going, weighed down with all the water I'll need for tonight and for the morning. I want to get myself out of today's dehydration hole, and I'm not confident that we'll be able to hike far enough to make it to another water source until tomorrow. Not with how tired Bugbite and I are, and definitely not with Gent's increasing pain, so I've packed out as much water as I can carry.

We cross a few roads, walking along the shoulder, following the trail markers that point us through a dirt parking lot and then directly uphill. The famed climb out of Breckenridge has now begun.

We hike into the early evening sun, pausing everywhere that looks even remotely flat so that we can assess its viability for three tents. We find a spot that kind of works, but it's a dirt road that might or might not get traffic coming through later tonight, so we decide to hike on. Gent has caught up with us now, and so we move together as a group, scoping out various little areas in the woods, our bodies dragging with fatigue, aware that we were all very ready to be done miles ago.

Eventually we find a spot, a grove of trees off to the side of another remote dirt road above the trail, and the relief I feel at finally being able to stop for the day is so very sweet. We pitch our tents close together, taking advantage of the flattest ground even though doing so means that we are almost on top of each other. But it works. We make it work. And being this close together feels cozy, comforting, safe.

I climb into my small shelter, doing our daily trail math. 17.8 miles, that's how far we hiked today. It feels like so much more than that, and yet all of my many aches seem to fade now that I am sitting down, now that I have wet-wiped my face, now that I've traded my sweaty hiking clothes for my soft fleece sleep top and wool leggings.

I sit like this, surrounded by all of my items the way I like to be, slowly spooning dinner into my mouth. I was unhappy before but now I'm not. The day felt agonizing and now it doesn't. It feels exactly right, being here. It feels like home.

◁ ▷

Day 7

The grove of trees around our tents acts as a shield against the wind, and I stay warm all night long. This warmth, combined with the fact that I was too dehydrated to get up and pee in the middle of the night means that by the time morning comes I feel well-rested and alert.

It's 6am, I am wide awake and gloriously energized, and yet I don't want to get out of my sleeping bag. It's cold now, the temperature started dropping just before dawn, and I haven't heard a single sound from either of the tents next to mine. No one wants to move, it seems.

"Hello?" I say quietly.

"Noooo," says Gent. "Not yet."

So I lay still and take advantage of the cell service in this spot, scrolling through Instagram, texting some friends, procrastinating on getting up, and eventually I look at the map to see what's ahead of us today. A big climb: that's what's ahead of us. Up up up up.

"How is it almost 8am?" I say, feeling frantic as I stuff the last of my things into my pack. Bugbite is long gone. Where did the morning go?

I hike alone for the next few hours, moving through the dewy woods, through a burn area, over and across the creeks and streams, my shoes squelching on the muddy trail. The air is smoky today, winds must have shifted in the night, which means I can't see anything out in the distance but at least my immediate surroundings are still clear and vibrant.

I find Bugbite mid-morning, sitting next to a flowing stream, and so I sit too, both of us eating weird little combinations of food from our packs. I alternate between fruit snacks and peanut butter; Bugbite is shoveling chip crumb remnants into their mouth with a spoon.

"I have been shitting so much," they say. "Multiple times a day, every day. And not, like, cute shits. Horrible shits. Awful, truly awful."

We try to analyze why this might be, eventually settling on our favorite explanation: that since Bugbite has had such a deeply grief-filled year, this massive expulsion is both an emotional and existential purging.

"Spiritual shits!" Bugbite says. "I am having spiritual shits!"

We each take one liter of water from the stream, filter it, pack up, and start hiking. Bugbite is off in front with their fast legs, and I'm doing my spoiled milk thing in the back. I find them again soon though, just past a sharp turn in the trail where they are standing still and laughing in an almost manic way as they point up at the steep mess of rocks that awaits us up ahead.

"What!" Bugbite cries, flailing both trekking poles all around, gesturing at how steep it is, how rocky, how unnervingly hard. "What what what!"

We don't know why this grueling section of trail seems so funny to us, but for some reason we cannot stop laughing. It is just so steep! We hike a few steps, gasp, laugh, hike laugh hike laugh. It's a long way to the top, watching our foot placement as we climb carefully up the talus fields, traversing along a rocky ridge.

We're up above 12,000 feet now, and my laughter has stopped. It's too high. I am on the twirly whirl—light-headed, slow, a little dizzy. I'm also coughing a lot, which is a new addition (smoke, maybe? or just the thin air?), and then all of the sudden my ghost hands are back, numb and useless at the ends of my arms. I look out at the hidden view before us, mountains invisible somewhere within the congested, smoky air, and I wonder if I will ever make it to the top of this climb. I mean, of course I will make it to the top, I always make it eventually, but why can't the top be now?

I hike slowly, keeping my eyes focused only on the section of dirt and rocks immediately in front of me, surrendering to moving upward for as long as it takes, following in Bugbite's footsteps. These individual steps add up until I am finally standing on top, a barren place with nothing but fierce wind, obscured views of the Ten Mile Range, and a cluster of large boulders into which Bugbite and I contort ourselves for a lunch break, hiding from the wind.

I put my rain jacket on, hood up, puffy coat spread across my lap like a blanket, trying to cover every inch of exposed skin. It is bitingly cold up here, and we each burrow into our own little rock nook, surrounded by our various items, making many jokes about how fucked it is that this is what we are choosing to do with our lives. I make myself eat while I wait for Gent even though I am still not hungry, still stuck with this frustrating nausea. But at least I am having fun! Who knew wedging oneself into a high-elevation rock pile could be such a good experience.

Gent shows up eventually, and his achilles tendon is in so much pain that he barely speaks to us. He just sits down and stares at the ground, barely eating, lost in the hell of his own body.

"Do you want to be alone?" I ask. He nods, and so Bugbite and I pack up and crawl out from the boulders, our bodies tipped forward into the wind. It's flat for a short while, exposed in every direction, 50+ mph gusts of air knocking us all around. Bugbite's rain pants flap loudly, billowing out like an inflated balloon, and together we begin the long descent, thousands of feet down down down into the woods toward Copper Mountain Resort where we have just learned (from another hiker) that there is apparently a restaurant only a few steps off trail but that this restaurant closes at 4pm. Will we make it? I don't think we can make it.

Gent catches up while we are refilling our water at a small stream. "Did you know about the restaurant?" I ask him. "Because the restaurant has burgers! Do you want a burger for dinner?"

This is my attempt to boost his morale; he just loves burgers so much. And the thought of a burger must outweigh the pain of whatever angry thing has taken up residence in his achilles, because as soon as I tell him about this new development he takes off. I mean he is just *gone*, flying down the trail, hitting the road, crossing the wooden bridge, taking off again into the woods. I hike as fast as I can, but I don't come close to catching him.

"They're open til 8!" he yells as I round the bend at the edge of a golf course near the resort. Not 4pm, 8pm. Jesus. We did not have to hike ourselves into the ground after all.

Copper Mountain is a ski resort, and we walk underneath the unmoving lifts, down the small hill from the trail to the brewery. There's some kind of concert happening on the grassy area in front—loud music, people dancing, other people sprawled out on blankets—a sensory overload compared to where we just came from. We get seated at an outdoor table, ignoring the highly inflated prices on the menu, and I order a black bean burger and onion rings, hoping that this new food will somehow be able to make it past my nausea filter.

The food arrives, and I watch as the others eat ravenously. They are so hungry! I should be hungry like this too, a week into a long-distance hike, but I am not. My appetite got left behind in Denver, I guess, and I mostly have to force myself to finish what I've ordered.

We hike out afterward, a heavy feeling in my gut, and I can tell right away that my body does not like this food. The trail goes uphill, and my body says to me, "Woman, listen, we can either digest onion rings or we can hike uphill but WE CANNOT DO BOTH." I almost throw up but don't. I almost emergency poop but don't. And so it is an endless slog to camp in which I am mostly miserable and yet I do not regret my choices. Onion rings? Who could ever regret onion rings. At least I finally ate something substantial, right?

It takes us until 7:40pm to find a flat enough spot to camp, off to the side of the trail overlooking a creek far below. The sun hasn't set but the temperature has already dropped at least 20 degrees, my fingers going numb in the cold air as I struggle to get all eight of my tent stakes into the ground. My only thought after that is burrowing—I just want to put on every single item of clothing I've got, crawl into my quilt, pull it up over my head, and hide, so I do.

I feel worried though, that it is already so cold and not even dark yet, but what can I do about it? Nothing. And I find that this "nothing" actually helps alleviate my worry, because if there is nothing to be done, what is the point of fretting about it? The only person who suffers if I worry all night about whether or not I will be too cold is me.

◁ ▷

Day 8

The frigid wind comes whipping through camp as soon as the sun has set, each gust easily finding its way into all of the flimsy mesh parts of my tent. At first I tell myself that it will stop, that of course it can't be *this* cold *all* night, and it turns out that I'm correct because it actually gets colder. Colder and colder, and I lay awake throughout the entire night wearing all of my layers, occasionally doing crunches from within my quilt, aiming to generate even a little bit of extra body heat. It works momentarily, but not enough to allow me to fall sleep, and so I am still awake when dawn breaks, curled on my side watching streaks of pink and orange bloom across the sky, the colors reflected in the misty creek down below.

As soon as the sun is up I'm moving, packing my gear away as quickly as I can, fingers numb, trying to pretend that I'm not already obliterated by exhaustion, feeling much too cold to eat anything. Mittens on, rain jacket on, buff pulled down around my ears, I pound up the trail by myself, stopping in each of the bright patches of morning light to turn my face upward, letting it warm my nose, my cheeks, my closed eyelids—the primal pleasure of the sun on your bare skin when you're freezing.

Slowly, my body warms up. Every step is gorgeous today, misty and green and vibrant and alive, and yet I keep getting stuck in pointless negative thought loops. I ruminate on an ex-friend and on why she ghosted me and on what it means about my inherent lovability if someone can be such a huge part of my life for years and years and then just suddenly disappear. My thoughts about this run around and around, followed by equally looping thoughts that are first about a decades-long family drama, and then about money scarcity, and then about all of the things I fear might be wrong or broken within me. Each time I catch myself doing this, falling into these loops, I try to use it as a chance to invite myself back to the present moment by naming five things I can see in front of me.

"Come back," I say to myself out loud. "What do you notice?"

Dark green spruce trees.

The flowing creek.

Hard-packed dirt trail underneath my feet.

Fields of tiny yellow wildflowers, hundreds and thousands of them blanketing the hillside.

Hazy smoke rolling slowly off in the distance.

It always grounds me, this noticing practice. But soon the seductive thought loops pull me back in, and then I do the noticing practice again, and then more thoughts and more noticing and more and more and on and on, back and forth throughout the entire morning.

Our brains, right? The wild little mess of being human.

It's in the throes of one of these thought loops that I suddenly realize, with alarming and terrifying urgency, that I am about to shit myself. The urge comes on so strong it's like I've been blindsided by a digestive freight train, the thought loops completely disintegrating as I run flat out toward a nearby cluster of trees and get there just in time to yank my shorts and underwear down, proceeding to have the kind of back-country pooping experience that I refer to as "digging the hole afterward." There is just absolutely no time to dig it beforehand, not when one is about to shit oneself.

So it's in this way that my previous thought spirals are put into perspective, because worrying about some stupid ex-friend drama seems much less pressing when I am squatting down in the woods, using a small, lightweight purple shovel to dig a hole in the dirt next to a pile of my own shit, using a pinecone to carefully move said shit into said hole, filling and covering the hole, putting my used toilet paper into a ziplock bag to throw out in town, and then liberally rubbing hand sanitizer into every crevice of my fingers.

Back on trail, I start the exposed ascent toward Kokomo Pass, and I soon find my friends, my little wolf pack, sitting at a cold stream. I filter water, add an electrolyte tablet, watch it bubble and fizz, eventually take some small sips while I dig through my food bag for anything that sounds even remotely appealing with my now ever-present nausea. I don't have any appetite at all today, and fruit snacks are the only thing I seem able to eat. I am concerned about this—more concerned than I have admitted to my hiking partners—truly and deeply worried that something is wrong with me, that I won't be able to complete this hike because of the nausea and the under-eating. These itty bitty fruit snacks cannot fuel a 500-mile hike.

Bugbite leaves the stream first, and Gent and I decide to do the rest of the climb together. We move slowly, fighting our way through my nausea and his achilles pain, getting ourselves up above tree line, hiking through the sprawling green slopes all the way to 12,000 feet, to Elk Ridge and the summit of Kokomo Pass. We are so high up that for a moment I feel astonished by it. You mean we can just... do this? We can just walk here, where it's so high and so beautiful? Smoke blocks our long-distance views but the immediate surroundings are green and bright, grasses and flowers blowing gently in the wind.

The descent is long and I hike it alone, listening to Twilight on audiobook, going down and down and down, thousands of feet down off the pass, knees aching, finally stopping under a wooden bridge near a waterfall where I soak a bandana and use it to wipe days of sweat from my face, groaning with gratitude as Gent takes the bandana and carefully cleans the worst of my searing back chafe for me as well.

I watch as the others eat lunch, Gent and Bugbite and another hiker, a 21-year-old guy named Danny, and I try to imagine myself eating what they are eating. Even the thought of it makes me gag, the back of my throat convulsing once, twice, three times, and I rest my head against the trunk of a tall tree and close my eyes. We sit there for over an hour in which my sour stomach and food aversion allows me to eat nothing but a handful of pretzels. That's it, just one small handful of pretzels. I frown, completely out of solutions to try to fix this problem that I have never had on any previous hike.

We leave the waterfall together, hiking in a little line, me at the back feeling sorry for myself. I am not hungry, but the lack of food must certainly be contributing to my low energy and even lower morale, right?

A person needs food, especially while hiking all day every day. What do I do about this, I wonder again and again. What do I do, what do I do, what do I do?

I zone out after that, turning into a hiking robot as I follow the footsteps of the people in front of me. They hike, so I hike too, almost as if I am attached to their backs by an invisible cord. The trail goes parallel to a dirt road, where every once in a while an ATV speeds by, submerging us in clouds of dust. We cross the road, hike along a flat stretch of trail to a place called Camp Hale where the remains of the 10th Mountain Division's WWII bunkers stand out against the otherwise undeveloped landscape. I am uninterested in this piece of history though, uninterested in literally everything except sitting down, which we finally do once we cross a nearby creek, tucking our bodies into the small amount of shade on the other side.

Cross-legged on the ground, still unable to eat, I cradle my head in my hands and close my eyes. It is so warm here. I am so sleepy. It feels like I could lay down for an hour, for a year, for the rest of my life. Just stay very still in this exact spot and let the earth reclaim me.

Enough, I think to myself. *I am going to turn this day around.* So I eat a bar, something with chocolate and nuts, and I swallow two tablets of ibuprofen. *I am going to turn this day around,* I think again. I am done feeling like steaming human garbage.

So I leave the shady spot before everyone else, and I hike, and I continue giving myself this little pep talk. I do this until the moment I feel the ibuprofen kick in, faster than I expected but I guess that's what happens when one is under-nourished and in a deep calorie deficit. Headache lifted, aches and pains gone, my morale shoots up toward the sky. Oh! Okay. Okay. I can do this. It's two and a half miles to the next water and I fly there, moving through the shade-dappled forest like an entirely different person from whoever I've been all day, taking no breaks, totally in flow, high on that rare feeling of hiking as poetry in motion.

I reach the water before the others, eyeing the nearby spot where we thought we were going to camp, but the ground isn't flat at all. How would we even sleep here?

"This place sucks," I call out to Gent and Bugbite as they arrive. "Think we can get a hitch into town tonight?"

It's late afternoon on a Sunday and we're currently four miles from the road. What time is sunset? How late in the evening do we think someone would pick us up? We debate this for a while as we keep checking our phones for cell service, to see if there are even any hotel rooms available in Leadville for tonight, but there's no service to be found and it's only getting later and later as we stand here in our uncertainty.

"Fuck it," I say. "I'm going."

I turn to leave and the others follow. We hike one mile, two miles, and it's then that I realize I never refilled my water at the last stop. I take a sip, one big sip, and then my bottle is empty. Oops?

"Oh well," I say, "I guess now I *need* to make it into town."

We hike a third mile and then a fourth mile and then we're there, 6:10pm on a Sunday night, thumbs out, hopeful smiles on our faces. 10 minutes go by, 20 minutes, 30 minutes. So many cars pass but none of them even slow down, except for a dude driving a flatbed truck with an open beer in his hand who says we can "ride on the back and just, like, hang on real tight." Uh, no thanks.

"Let's keep trying until 7pm," Bugbite says. "If no one stops we can stealth camp over in those trees and try again in the morning."

This idea is deeply unappealing to me, now that I'm out of water and the desire for the luxuries of town has taken root in my heart.

6:45pm, 6:50pm, nothing.

But at 6:56pm a small car pulls over, two older folks and a dog named Pippi. We scramble into the back, smooshing our three bodies together with our packs on our laps, exclaiming our gratitude over and over and over again.

It takes about 20 minutes to get down from the pass, and they drop us at the edge of town. Bugbite gets a hotel room and Gent and I split a second room, splurging so that everyone can have their own bed. I shower, eat a foot-long sandwich from Subway while still wrapped in my towel, and then I spread out like a starfish on the soft white bed, not planning to move another inch for the entire night.

◁ ▷

Day 9

What's that saying about how the reason you keep hitting yourself with a hammer is because of how good it feels when you finally stop? That's a zero day on a thru-hike.

I wake up in my squish hotel bed, go to the bathroom in a flushing toilet, wash my hands with actual soap, procure earl grey tea and a big blueberry muffin from the local coffee shop, eat it all in bed, refuse to leave the bed. Bed bed bed. Eventually it's checkout time, and we pack up our things and wander over to a cafe called the Silver Llama for breakfast.

Kelsey, my friend and former partner who I haven't seen in almost 7 years, drives up from Denver to meet us at this cafe, and it is so good to see him. It is also so good (like, miraculously world-changingly good) to find something at this cafe (avocado caprese toast) that I am not entirely repulsed by eating. It's like the opposite of hiker hunger, whatever has been happening to me. I keep thinking about it, about how I should be craving *more* food by this point in the hike, not less, and yet I seem to want no food at all. Yesterday I started cutting back on the Diamox dosage—maybe that will help? Maybe it's not the altitude that is making me sick but the medication I am taking to prevent altitude sickness? How bullshit would that be.

I make it through my whole breakfast though, eating every single bite, and that feels like a huge victory. From there it's resupply boxes from the post office, checking into our new room at the local hostel, a big room with multiple beds—one each for me, Gent, and Bugbite, plus a bed for my friend Emily who gets into town tonight and will hike with us for the next few days.

At the hostel we explode our gear everywhere, sort through everything, clean everything, fall into our phones. I spend a while looking at maps of the upcoming section, at the steeper elevation profile ahead, before we all walk over to the pizza place for lunch where I order a spinach salad and a big plate of focaccia bread with marinara dipping sauce. I eat slowly, mostly not hating this food but still feeling a little nauseated, and afterward Gent and I go to Melanzana, the little shop in the center of Leadville whose micro-fleece hoodies have gained a cult-like following amongst thru-hikers. Gent has wanted one of these hoodies for years and years, but they don't sell them online and right now you need an appointment to shop in-person, and even then you are limited to buying just two items. He buys one hoodie for himself and one for Bugbite, who couldn't get an appointment, and I buy one for me and one for my friend Kelly. We put them on as we walk out of the store, Gent's joyful face lit up like a Christmas tree the whole way back to the hostel.

It's late afternoon now, just past 4:30pm, and I take off all my clothes and wrap myself in a towel while

Gent goes to put our laundry in the washing machine next door. My bottom bunk bed has a thin curtain all around it and I pull it closed, tucking myself under the covers. Bugbite pulls their curtain closed as well, and a soft and comforting silence spreads across the room. Tomorrow it's back to the mountains and the purple wildflowers and the bright bright stars. But for now? We nap.

◁ ▷

Day 10

There's a saying out here, that "the trail provides", and here's how that happens for me today:

Emily arrived last night, and first thing this morning she lets me borrow her car so I can drive all the way back to Denver, to where my van is parked, so that I can get my warmer sleeping bag. I've been strategizing about this for the past few days now, about what the hell to do about these freezing cold nights, knowing that if I can't get warm I will continue to lay awake all night, which when combined with the fact that I am also underfed has left me feeling like a shell of a person. So while I am slightly resentful of having to interrupt my hike with a spontaneous multi-hour roadtrip I know that it is an exceptionally worthwhile choice, a choice that Future Me will be so grateful about.

Gent comes with me—he wants to grab his stove from the van (it's his first time cold-soaking and in these temperatures he has just about had it with that), and we also need to stop at REI to buy a new water filter for Bugbite and some warmer sleep clothes for Gent. I'll need to get a compression sack too, because otherwise there's no way my huge floof sleeping bag is fitting into my small frameless pack. So we get on the road, Gent driving us down from the mountains, me picking at my spinach and feta croissant, and somehow it only takes a little over two hours to drive what it just took us 9 days to hike, and that feels... yeah. But we're able to do all of our errands, and as soon as we've been below 6,000 feet for about 30 minutes I find that I feel so much better. No nausea at all, proper hunger, strong food cravings, as if someone has flicked a wellness switch on inside my body.

Okay, I think, making note of this interesting development. Maybe it has indeed been the elevation all along? But I also stopped taking Diamox last night, so maybe it's that as well? I think about it as I take my turn behind the wheel after we've completed our errands, driving us back up into the mountains and waiting for the moment when I begin to feel sick again, and all too soon, once we're above 9,000 feet, there it is. Crap.

Back in Leadville I make a quick trip to Subway, buying myself a large veggie-filled sandwich, hoping I'll want to eat that more than any of my cold-soaked options for dinner tonight. It's 2pm when we finally get dropped off at the trailhead, me and Gent and Bugbite and Emily, and I struggle to try and fit all of my stuff into my pack before we head out. The compression sack helps to make the big sleeping bag more manageable, but it still takes up noticeably more space than the quilt I swapped it out for, and so between that and my restocked food bag, plus the Subway sandwich and family-size bag of white cheddar popcorn I have stubbornly insisted on bringing for this section, it's a tight fit. My solution is to throw one of my water bottles in the trailhead trashcan so that I can use that same spot in my pack's side pockets for my sandwich, which means that yes I am gambling with my hydration over a damn sandwich, but here we are. I then strap the popcorn to the very top of the pack, extend my trekking poles to their proper length, make sure my shoes are tied, and follow my friends into the woods.

We hike together for a little while, but it doesn't take long until I need to stop and pee, after which I fall behind. I don't mind though; after the hectic nature of our roadtrip detour it feels soothing to hike alone in the cool forest, listening to my favorite music, know-ing my friends are off in front of me somewhere and that eventually our paths will converge again.

The trail is rocky, but the forest is shaded and I cross over creeks and streams that are rushing and plentiful, a comforting sight now that I am down a water bottle and will need to fill up more frequently. Throughout the afternoon our little group comes together and splits up, depending on the steepness of the climbs. The terrain definitely feels more challenging now, on this side of Tennessee Pass, but the views at the top are worth it—big boulders and funky rock slabs, clear skies, thick green trees, colorful mushrooms of all types, everything a mix of texture and color and bursting with a pulsing feeling of aliveness.

It's buggy though, mosquitos flying all around, landing on my face and arms and legs whenever I slow down, so I forgo almost every urge to rest and take a break. We finally stop around 7:30pm, 11 miles away from where we started this afternoon, making camp on a slightly sloped spot near a small lake where I sit in my tent and eat my entire sandwich and some big handfuls of pop-corn without feeling sick, without gagging even once, and this feels like monumental progress.

After that I burrow down into my 10-degree Western Mountaineering sleeping bag, and it's honestly like

I'm laying inside of a cloud, like I could never possibly be cold ever again. *Oh thank god*, I think, peering out the mesh of my tent as the very last of the day's light slips away behind the trees, temperature dropping steadily in its wake.

The air is completely still now, no breeze, no sounds, nothing at all but the peaceful night and the thump thump of my grateful heart, beating strong and steady inside my chest.

◁ ▷

Day 11

I sleep well in my squish cloud sleeping bag, and in the morning as I lay there and procrastinate on getting up by looking at the maps for today I realize just how badly I am going to need this well-rested energy, because ohhhh boy here we go today, strapping into the rollercoaster of elevation change.

I pack my gear slowly, listening to Gent's recap of what the night was like over in his tent, a non-stop nosebleed and an upturned water bottle that has completely soaked the inside of one of his shoes. Bugbite leaves camp first and I get going myself a while later, leaving Emily and Gent to play caboose on our little hiker train this morning.

The trail pitches upward directly out of camp, a climb so steep that I stop three times in half a mile to lean my forehead on my trekking poles, convinced I'm going to black out. This is much too efforty for first thing in the morning, I think. Much much too efforty. So I go slow, cresting the top and then following the trail as it takes a sharp downward turn, worrying about Gent's achilles as I hike. He had hoped that it would be better after the day and a half of rest in Leadville, but no. All of yesterday afternoon he was plagued by it, trying not to complain but I could read the pain all across his face.

There is nothing you can do for him in this moment, I remind myself, and so I take a few deep breaths, get grounded, and give myself permission to get lost in the flow of the trail, moving alone through the woods, and as I hike and hike I slip into a sort of trance. My legs are strong, the breeze is cool and gentle, and for an hour I am filled with the sense that I could hike literally anything this trail were to put in front of me. I don't feel this kind of invincibility too often, but when I do it makes every hard moment out here feel totally and completely worth it.

Emily and Bugbite are already at the stream when I get there for lunch, and I throw down my pack, sweaty and starving. It finally happened this morning: I am hungry again! The altitude monster who stole my appetite for the past 10 days has suddenly relinquished it, and now I want to just eat and eat. I sit on the ground and devour oatmeal with chocolate chips, big handfuls of white cheddar popcorn, a cold liter of electrolyte water with fruit punch mixed in. I take my sweat-soaked shirt off and spread it out to dry in the sun, lay on the ground with my legs up a tree, resting as I wait for Gent. He should be here by now, right? I check the time. He should definitely be here by now.

I'm ready to leave when he eventually shows up, absolutely wrecked with pain, and it breaks my heart to see him like this. I extend my lunch break to keep him company, watching as Emily and Bugbite hike off without us, worried looks on both their faces.

Gent doesn't talk much, eating slowly with tears in his eyes. He's had achilles issues on past hikes, but nothing like this.

"Why is this happening," he says, anguished. "I trained for this hike! I thought I was so strong."

I stay by his side for the rest of the afternoon, hiking as slowly as he needs to go, taking lots of hug breaks and stretch breaks, loading him up on ibuprofen, discussing our options.

"I will support whatever you want to do," I say. And I mean it.

We find our friends at a stream six miles down the trail, and it's clear that they've been waiting for us for quite a while.

"I'm sorry I'm so slow," Gent says to them, eyes cast downward at the trail, and of course they brush that off. He doesn't need to apologize, and yet I know exactly how he feels—it is agonizing to be the injured one, the slowest one, the one who constantly feels as if they are holding everyone else back. I have been that person multiple times before, so I get it. Oh god do I get it.

The climb away from the stream is steep and switchbacked, and Gent asks us all to go out ahead of him.

"The uphills are the worst," he says. "I just want to be alone in the back."

It's not that far to camp though, luckily, where we all pitch our tents in a small clearing near a rushing creek and finalize a plan for what comes next.

"I think I need to quit," Gent says.

He and I talked about this at length all afternoon, and I was pretty sure he was leaning this way, but I still feel gutted to actually hear him say it. Every single thru-hike attempt he has made over the past six years, since spring of 2015, has ended sooner than he wanted for one reason or another, and I know how badly he was hoping that this trail, this hike, this year, would be different.

"Yeah," he says, voice a bit steadier, "I am going to quit."

There isn't much to say after that, and we each finish setting up our tents in the quiet evening, pulling out various food items and readying ourselves to make dinner.

Should I quit, too? This is the question that's been running on a loop in my mind for the past few hours—even though Gent and I talked about this exact possibility before setting out, about what we'd do if one of us needed to stop for a non-emergency reason, and in that conversation we agreed that the other person should keep hiking if they wanted to keep hiking. And yeah, as selfish as it makes me feel in this moment, I want to keep hiking. But should I? I don't know.

We sit in a circle in front of our tents for dinner, watching and laughing as Emily adds an almost obscene amount of butter to her mac and cheese. She packed out a full stick of butter (!) for just two nights (!!) of backpacking with us, and even though we've been teasing her about that since leaving Leadville it now appears as though she's indeed going to finish the whole thing.

"Your trail name can be Full Stick," Gent says, smiling.

"FULL STICK!" we all yell, laughing and smiling as well.

We eat together after that, and while we eat, we talk, and the plan we decide upon is this:

Gent will leave with Emily tomorrow morning, at the road crossing where her brother is coming to pick her up, and I will keep hiking with Bugbite. Emily, wonderful friend that she is, has already called her local connections, booking Gent in with a PT who specializes in working with endurance athletes. So he'll rest, ice, and then get PT treatment, and maybe after that he'll be able to rejoin us on trail.

I think about this as I tuck myself into my fluff sleeping bag after dinner, about how much I'll miss him and how sudden his departure feels, and yet I am grateful for the choice he's making, that he's doing what's best for his body in this moment, that he is humble enough to be able to choose long-term health and well-being over everything else, even if he has to break his own heart in order to do it.

◁ ▷

Day 12

I must have slept with my mouth hanging open all night, because when I wake up my throat and tongue and gums are so dry that I feel like a zombie, as if my mouth has been replaced with a dead and desiccated zombie mouth, as if I will never be able to produce saliva or swallow anything ever again.

I press my lips together, try to move my tongue across each of my teeth and run it along the roof of my mouth, and oh my god it tastes like a zombie mouth too. I chug some water, cough, little droplets flying all over my chest and my sleeping bag—time to get up.

I slept well last night, probably about 7 straight hours, lulled by the sounds of the babbling creek and the warmth of my squish sleeping bag. I start to pack up, feeling so good and well-rested that it takes me a few minutes to remember that Gent is leaving us today. Everyone else is quiet too, mood somber as we get our things together and leave camp a little before 8am.

"Can we stay together today?" I ask. Emily and Gent are leaving so soon, at the road crossing in a few hours, and I want to enjoy every second of their company for as long as I can.

We file into a line, the trail taking us up a short climb but then it's all downs and flats toward Twin Lakes, the perfect terrain for talking with one's friends. The closer we get the more signs of civilization we see— RVs and pit toilets and picnic tables, day hikers and mountain bikers too.

The road crossing comes even sooner than I expected, and it's there that we find Jameson, Emily's brother, already parked in the little pullout, waiting. Gent and Emily put their packs in the trunk of the car, walking back around to hug me and then Bugbite.

"This feels so weird," I say to Gent. "Like, you're just gonna get in that car and I'll keep hiking?"

"I know," he says, crying a little. "I don't want to leave you."

"My beloved," I say, running a finger down his cheek.

"The love of my life," he responds, resting his forehead against mine.

"Thank you for taking care of my person!" I call out to Emily as she climbs into the passenger seat of the car, Gent reluctantly opening the rear door and getting in after her.

Everyone waves as they drive away, and then Bugbite and I look at each other, the last two left.

"So I suppose we should keep hiking?" Bugbite says.

"Yeah," I say. "There's nothing else we can do."

We walk along the flat hot trail, which now runs parallel to both the highway and the lake, no shade. Eventually we find a spindly little tree, and we take a mid-morning break under its branches, pretending that this does anything at all to block out the bright heat of the sun. I eat oatmeal, grateful all over again to still be feeling so hungry, and then I stretch, trying to alleviate the heavy leg feeling that has settled in throughout the day.

Eventually the trail takes us across a dam, on the other side of which we are almost immediately back in the woods where my body seems to sigh in relief. The trees! I love the trees. The cooler air! No more feeling exposed to so many cars and so many people. We take another short break, eat chips, talk about how daunted we feel by the impending climb up and over Hope Pass, which the map tells us is just mile after mile of relentless up, gaining thousands of feet in too short of a time.

10.5 miles into the day and we hit an important trail junction, one where hikers get to do a choose-your-own adventure route selection for the Collegiate Peaks area. We can either follow the original Colorado Trail route (Collegiate East) or the supposedly harder, higher, prettier, and slightly longer Collegiate West. We go west.

It's a little under four miles from there to the start of the climb, and although Bugbite and I stay together we are quiet, each hiking in our own internal worlds. I stop to drain a blister on my heel, sanitizing my little needle with an antiseptic wipe, watching the fluid dribble out and run down the side of my foot. I put a dab of antibiotic ointment on it, roll my dirty sock back on and wiggle into my shoe, delighted by how much better it feels to have that pressure released. And it's just in time too, because here we are at the base of the ascent.

The ascent. I feel like I am already wilting in the heat, in the thick humidity, and as I stare after Bugbite who has started moving up the rocky incline all I can think is that I do not want to hike over this pass. I do not, I do not, I do not. I am hot. I am sad. I miss Gent. Nothing sounds worse than this right now.

But the thing about a thru-hike (the thing I love so much) is that while it is not easy it is simple. I deeply do not want to hike up 3,500 feet over the next 3.8 miles, but my choice is either to do it or to quit. That's it: you go forward or you quit, and I know that I do not want to quit, so I begrudgingly put one foot in front of the other as I slowly start climbing up the rock strewn trail.

You do not have to be in the mood to do something in order to do it, I remind myself.

And it's true, I don't. So instead I go into business mode: I'm just here to put in work. Three quarters of a mile up, tie my hair back, filter some cold cold water from the creek, chug, put my bottle back in the side pocket of my pack, wipe my sweaty face with my sweaty shirt, smearing the sweat and dirt all around. Another half mile up, another short rest, commit to doing whatever it takes to keep splitting the rest of this climb into tiny manageable sections. Another mile up, sit in the dirt with my head in my hands, every inch of my body coated with sweat. Are my eyeballs sweating? It feels like they are. Stand up; hike more; sit in the dirt more; hike more; reach the next water source to find that it's dry; fall into manic, adrenaline-fueled laughter with Bugbite about how we're both almost out of water and so of course the stream is dry and oh god it feels like we have always been climbing Hope Pass and that we will always be climbing Hope Pass, forever and onward.

"My shin hurts," Bugbite says as we drag ourselves back to standing. "Whatever this shin splint thing is that's been going on for a few days, it really hurts."

We hike on, water bottles soon completely empty, until we finally pop out above tree line and wow, yes, wow, okay. If you want the majestic, mind-bending views you must hike and hike and hike for them, I remember that now.

The higher we go the more the cold wind whips across our faces, keeping the swarms of biting bugs at bay, which have otherwise been attacking us all afternoon. The last half mile of the climb is so hard, just devastatingly hard, but it's perfect too—the air is clear, there's no smoke in sight, no rain clouds, and I get myself to the top by chanting "perfect, lucky, perfect, lucky" over and over again.

At the top the wind encircles us, forces us to keep our snack break short, get started on the massive descent down the other side. I do not like descending—for as hard as the climbs can be they aren't nearly as rough on my body, don't give my joints the same beating and pounding, and so I take tiny mincing steps along the slippery gravel as the descent begins, determined to stay upright as we make our way together down toward the trees once more. We can make it all the way down before dark, right? We've gotta try.

"So you know my friends in Oregon with the toddler?" I say to Bugbite while we descend and descend.

"Yeah," Bugbite says. "What about them?"

"The toddler, Aida, she does this thing when she has fucking *had it* with something, where she names that thing and then shouts 'ANYMORE' after it. So like, if she's bundled up in a jacket and she's starting to sweat she will yell, 'JACKET ANYMORE' until you help her take it off."

Bugbite laughs, turning around to look at me, unsure of where this is going.

"My knees," I moan. "DESCENDING ANYMORE!!"

I swallow down some ibuprofen at the final water source of the evening, the stream we find right before a sort-of-flat-enough spot off in the woods. We can't pitch our tents next to each other, the only two flat-ish spots are a good ways apart, but we don't care. We'll take it. We are not hiking another step tonight.

"I feel disgusting" I say as Bugbite walks over to my tent with their food bag and butt pad. "I think I sweat more today than on this entire trail put together so far."

We cold-soak our various bean mixtures, spooning the resulting brown (me) and green (Bugbite) "meals" into our mouths. I eat every single bite—the beans, the rice, the chips, I even remember to dump the olive oil packet on top of it all for extra fat and calories. And this, the fact that my hunger is not a fluke, that I am feeling better, that I can eat normally again, it is such a relief. Maybe I will be able to hike this whole trail after all!

Bugbite stretches after dinner, trying to ease their shin pain. They fold up into a version of child's pose, torso on thighs, whimpering.

"This is the worst yoga class of my life," they say.

When darkness comes we each crawl into our own shelters. I get into my cloud-like sleeping bag, pull it up to my chin, waiting for all that floof to warm my body, hoping that once I'm warm the warmth will compensate for all the little zings I feel in my muscles and tendons. I am really sore tonight!

21 miles, I think. We walked and walked and went up and up and down and down, moving ourselves another

21 miles today. Is that a lot of miles? Is it not enough? I find that I cannot conceptualize the meaning of anything right now.

Sleep, I tell myself. Probably you just need to sleep.

◁ ▷

Day 13

6:45am and I'm exhausted, having only slept for an hour or so at a time all night, and yet somehow I must now get up and do it all again. My legs are not even remotely recovered from yesterday's steep pass, and as I squat down to take my tent stakes out of the ground this morning it feels like a kind of death.

But I've learned not to make how I feel when I first get up mean anything about the day ahead, trusting that as I hike my body will warm up and everything will be fine.

"You just need to wake up the muscles," I say out loud to myself, slapping my palms against my thighs in an effort to rally them to the cause. Just gotta wake 'em up!

Recovered or not, I feel absolutely thrilled to be hiking today. You mean I just get to wander through the quiet nature for hours and hours and hours, all day long? What. How. Okay! I zip my fanny pack shut, leaving camp right behind Bugbite, and as we hike we alternate between talking and just moving silently through the forest. There are streams and creeks and rivers, flowing and cascading over boulders and fallen trees, water water everywhere.

My legs soon feel better, morale is high, and by 10am we have officially hiked 200 miles. I think about this as I slowly climb up toward Lake Ann Pass, about how insignificant it feels to hike from one snack break to the next each day, but look! 200 miles. It all adds up.

I feel so proud of myself, sweating hard as the trail takes me above tree line where I stop mid-stride and just stare and stare in all directions. A moment ago I was in the dense woods, but now I am standing in the middle of what feels like a bowl of mountains, jagged and towering peaks rising up on all sides of me, the sparkling blue-green water of the lake down below.

Shortly after that the trail disappears, our route becoming a series of sharp fields of talus, up up up, a few spots that trigger my panicky fear of heights, but eventually there is no more up and it is utterly majestic at the top.

I sit on the ground, feeling a slight elevation headache but only barely, realizing I haven't taken any ibuprofen yet today. No more Diamox, very little ibuprofen, I must finally be acclimating!

Bugbite, on the other hand, is not doing so well, sitting quietly and poking their painful shin splint spot, a worried look on their face.

We stay like that for a while, absorbed in the view and in our own inner worlds, and when we finally start the descent it isn't nearly as bad as I feared. It helps that we're going into town tomorrow, which means that my food bag is almost empty and my pack is feather light, so light that I find myself almost skipping down the trail in some of the flatter spots.

Soon we're back in the woods, the afternoon air cool and misty, everything dripping wet and mossy in a way I've only ever seen in the Pacific Northwest. Bugbite falls behind, nursing their shin, and I start to worry that they will need to quit as well, that despite starting with two other people I will eventually wind up out here all alone. I try not to think about it.

An hour passes, a thunderstorm rolls in, and we wait it out in a little nook of fallen trees with two other hikers, a couple who we haven't met before.

"I'd like to stop soon," Bugbite says once we're able to resume hiking. "I am really hurting."

So we hike across the damp fresh earth into the early evening, scanning for a good spot, water droplets splattered on every branch and leaf and wisp of bright green moss. The trail is pretty flat here, and it must be some kind of ranching land because what I thought was mud is actually cow shit, piles and piles of it all along the trail, smeared across the bottoms of our shoes.

We hike slowly until about 5pm, until we reach a grassy spot, a meadow of sorts that's close to water and not completely covered in cow shit, and we pitch our tents so that the doors face each other. It's early, the earliest we've stopped in a while, and it feels luxurious to have so much time at camp. We stretch, we eat our little cold-soaked jars of food, we talk about Bugbite's worsening shin splint pain.

"I don't know what to do," they say. "Maybe I should take a few days off?"

The temperate drops as soon as the sun goes down, and I eat fistfuls of chocolate chips while cocooned inside my sleeping bag. I feel terrible for Bugbite and have no idea what they are going to decide, but I try to put it out of my mind. For now I am warm and dry, the pastel colors of sunset are unfurling, eclipsing the last of the rain clouds beyond the trees, and in focusing on this I am able to let it all go, the worries, the "what's next", all of it. Because the truth is that if I allow my mind to be here, to be right where my body is, it's wonderful—a singularly soft and gentle kind of bliss.

◁ ▷

Day 14

I wake up at 3:30am, hips and glutes aching from all the elevation change over the past few days, the normal discomforts of a long-distance trek. Otherwise I have been sleeping mostly okay out here, much better than on previous hikes, so as I thrash around on my sleeping pad trying to find a more comfortable position I am confident that I'll soon fall back asleep.

I do, and when dawn comes I wake to a damp sleeping bag and a tent that is soaked with condensation. All of my things are wet, but there are only 6.6 miles between here and the highway and that highway leads to pancakes and pancakes are all that I've been thinking about for weeks now, so who even cares about wet gear. Pancakes pancakes pancakes!

The mental image of these pancakes, stacked high and smothered in melted butter and warm maple syrup, that image fuels me with both delight and the total agony of anticipation. So distracted am I by these food fantasies that it takes me until I am almost done packing up, until all my wet things are stashed away, to realize that Bugbite is quieter than usual.

"How are you feeling today?" I ask, looking over at where they are standing outside their tent, staring off into the distance.

"I don't know," they say. "I don't think I've been honest with myself about how much pain I'm in, but it's really bad."

We talk about this as we hike out, about the emotional process of deciding on the next best step. Is it dangerous to push through? Better to rest for a few days? Stop hiking entirely? I have made each of these choices myself on various past hikes, and none of them felt easy.

After a while the conversation fades, each of us meandering through our own thoughts as we continue to move down the trail, which is mostly flat for a couple miles, muddy and slick, and I balance precariously on two separate log crossings as I will myself not to fall into either of the cold creeks below.

As I walk I try to assess my own feelings in reaction to what Bugbite is working through. How do I feel about hiking alone for a few days? Given how much ibuprofen Bugbite has been taking, do I really think they'll be able to rejoin me? Do I think Gent will be able to rejoin me? Is this all just leading to the inevitable moment when I need to decide whether or not to hike the remaining 270+ miles all by myself? That would be okay, right? I could do it?

Soon we reach the base of the climb up to Cottonwood Pass, which our map says is the spot where we'll find a trailhead parking lot and a road that leads down the mountain into town. From the place where we camped last night to that road it's only 6.6 miles, and this low mileage has fooled me into thinking that it will be an easy morning. 6.6 miles is nothing. I can hike 6.6 miles.

And sure, yes, of course I can do it, but oh my god is it steep. Right from the start this climb is intense in a way that I am not prepared for, the relentless feeling of gaining 1,000 feet in just the first mile alone.

I stop often, taking lots of micro breaks, breaks that are just long enough for me to catch my breath, wipe at the sweat that's dripping down my chest and pooling into my sports bra. I eat all of my remaining food, every last thing I've got, and as I hike I feel the untamed hunger that claws at my belly.

Eventually we decide to rest for real, by the side of a stream where we can sit on the damp earth and filter half a liter of water into our bottles. This is the last water stop, and that's all we should need to make it to the top.

"I feel so heartbroken about getting off trail," Bugbite says, filtering the water. "I'm just so disappointed and sad."

They cry as they talk, and I notice that the more outwardly emotional they become the more I can feel my own walls going up, keeping their pain at a greater and greater distance, somehow unable to hold space for it while I also try to parse through my own vulnerability at being left alone out here. I tell myself that I should be able to do both—be a true comfort to my friend and also to myself—and yet in this moment it seems that I do not have the capacity for both at the same time.

Does this mean that I am selfish? That I am a bad friend? I think about it as I continue to hike, soon breaking through the trees as the trail continues to climb and climb, moving ever upward, and I try to be here, to be right where my feet are, to remember that in this moment I am still with my friend, surrounded by lush green mountains and clear blue skies, sun shining brightly, glistening off the last of the day's remaining dew drops.

There's one more short, steep ascent and then we're there, standing at the road with our thumbs out, and the first vehicle that approaches pulls right over for us, a retired math teacher in an RV who takes us to the breakfast spot in town. There's a long wait, my mounting hunger seems to stretch time out in all directions, but eventually we get seated and there is tea and orange juice and hash browns and bacon and pancakes. Finally: the pancakes. I devour it all.

We decide to get a motel in town for the night, instead of the original plan of resupplying and hitching right back to trail, because now that Bugbite has decided to quit for good, not just take a few days off, we want a little more time together. So we shower, we do laundry, and I wander through the aisles of the grocery store trying to decide what I might want to eat for the next few days. This is the only town where I haven't mailed myself a box of food, because it's only two and a half days until the next stop in Salid, and two days of food should be easy to buy, right? But no. The decision fatigue I feel as I try to do calorie math to determine whether or not I'm buying enough is overwhelming, especially when combined with the effort of trying to choose at least a few things of nutritional value.

"It's just two days," I eventually say to myself. "Who cares about nutritional value. Buy whatever the hell you want."

So I do, and the end result of all my items spread out across the checkout counter looks like a 6-year-old has been left unsupervised at a birthday party. Candy! Oreos! Cheetos and chocolate bars and fruit punch and Spaghetti O's!

Back at the motel I talk to Gent on the phone as I stuff this food into my pack, smiling at my choices. I am so excited to eat all of these things!

"So I saw the PT today," Gent says.

"Yeah?"

"Yeah."

"And?" I ask.

"This hike is definitely over for me."

We're both quiet for a moment, letting that sink in. Bugbite is done. Gent is done.

"I want to stay out here with you though," he says. "Assuming you want to keep hiking? I've got your van now, I can meet up with you and bring you lots of trail magic? We can hang out in town together when you resupply?"

Everything he says sounds like it has a question mark at the end, and I realize that's because he's waiting for me to decide. Do I want to keep going? It would be so much easier to quit, right? To be done now that everyone else is done. Should I stop too? Would that be the more supportive thing? Will Gent really have fun driving around rural Colorado, meeting me at random backcountry trailheads, supporting me on a trek that he so badly wants to be doing himself?

The questions swirl around my mind, faster and faster and faster and faster, until all of the sudden it all goes quiet. There is no more mental chatter. No more wondering. No more questions. There is only this:

The pure feeling of my own heart, the bright certainty of knowing that I do not want to quit.

"I am not quitting," I say to Gent, selfish as it might be. "I love you, I'm so grateful you're going to support me as I hike, and I can't wait to see you in Salida in two days."

◁ ▷

Day 15

I lay awake for most of the night, mind racing, the small light of the microwave clock and of the power button on the TV seeming to glow brighter and brighter with every hour that passes.

I listen to Bugbite's even breathing as I thrash from one position to another, unable to let go of the fear I feel about hiking out alone tomorrow, of the potential thunderstorm that's forecasted to start just after 4pm, of how it will feel to go back up into the high mountains without either of the people that I started this adventure with.

I can do this, right? I can keep going on my own? I felt confident enough yesterday but nighttime is my fear time, as if my self-belief can't outlast the setting sun, so now here I am in the middle of the night, blankets pulled up over my head to block out those incessant little lights, feeling anxious, breathing too fast, lost in wave after wave of doubt.

I fall asleep eventually, sometime just before dawn, but then all too soon the alarm is blaring and I run around the motel room grabbing all of my exploded gear. Everything fits in my pack except the big bag of puffy Cheetos, which I am determined not to leave without, so I dump as many of them as I can into a gallon-size ziplock instead, strap it to the top of the pack, and cinch it down tight. I might not know what's ahead of me today but at least I'll have plenty of cheesy snacks.

Bugbite and I walk to a nearby cafe where I order a thick green smoothie with an extra scoop of protein powder, plus the biggest and most caffeinated tea on the menu. I take alternating sips of both on the walk back to the motel, grabbing my bag and standing outside to wait for Barbara, the trail angel who has kindly agreed to give me a ride back up to Cottonwood Pass at 8am.

She arrives right on time, and I feel dazed as I quickly hug Bugbite goodbye, toss my pack on the back seat, and buckle myself in beside Barbara. Bugbite and I wave to each other through the window until the car turns and I can't see them anymore, until it is just me and Barbara, driving up the endlessly windy pass, the nausea of car sickness flooding my body, exacerbated by the nerves I feel about spending the entire day hiking alone above tree line.

"Thanks so much!" I call to Barbara as she backs out of the parking lot with her windows rolled down.

"Be safe!" she says, flipping on her turn signal and beginning the drive back down the mountain.

I watch her leave, checking the time on my phone. 8:30am, back at Cottonwood Pass, alone. Okay, I think, time to hike.

I lean into the short, steep climb that takes me away from the parking lot, passing the couple of day hikers who must have started just before me, little droplets of sweat already breaking out across my forehead and slipping down the sides of my face. I reach the top and see the trail winding out in front of me, a thin ribbon of dirt and rocks that twists across the landscape of green and jagged peaks. The sky is a vibrant, crystalline blue right now, this afternoon's projected storm nowhere in sight, and I stand there for a moment and spread my arms out wide, realizing that the only thing I need to do now is walk. That is it. Just walk. And walk.

I move across the trail, thrumming with an unexpectedly vibrant energy. Being alone is incredible! After days (weeks?) of perpetually worrying about other people—about their injuries, their mental state, the morale of the group, what everyone needs, which campsites are big enough for all of us—it is an utter relief to be alone, to feel free, to revel in the selfish thrill of doing only and exactly what I want.

I hike for one hour, two hours, three hours, no breaks, morale soaring through all of these miles and miles of unencumbered aloneness. I traverse up and down the many steep and pointed passes that make up this completely exposed section of trail, a section where there is no tree cover at all, where I am kept mostly above 12,000 feet all morning long, hiking through a minor elevation headache, eyes feasting on the expansive way the trail stays visible so far into the distance now that nothing else is there to block the view.

As noon approaches and the sun beats down I start to look for a patch of shade, somewhere that I can stop for a while, eat lunch, maybe rest for an hour or so. There aren't many options, as exposed as it is, so I do my best to contort myself into the one small pocket of quasi-shade I can find. Shoes off, socks off, sitting cross legged on my little foam pad, eating handfuls of Cheetos as I contentedly zone out, my gaze growing soft and fuzzy. Eventually I dig out my full food bag, coaxing myself to eat something more substantial, feeling the soreness in my legs and realizing that I forgot to refill my ibuprofen in town after giving almost all of it to Bugbite in the last section. There are just four tablets left now, and I frown as I stare at them in my hand. How could I have forgotten to restock something so crucial? I beat myself up about this for a while, until I stretch my legs out and in doing so quickly glance back the way I came, up toward Cottonwood Pass where the sky has started to darken with clouds.

I check the time on my phone, suddenly frantic. The storm wasn't supposed to start until after 4pm today, and it's only 12:10 right now. How far away are those clouds? Which direction are they moving? I pack quickly, shoving my uneaten food and four remaining tablets of ibuprofen back where they came from, trying not to panic but completely unsure of how scared I should actually be. I have never been above tree line in a storm before. There is nowhere nearby that I could drop down and take proper cover from the threat of lightning if I needed to, absolutely nowhere at all. Shit. Shit shit.

Stop, I think. *Breathe.*

The sky above me is still blue. The sky in the direction I am headed is clear. The storm is behind me, so I will just begin hiking, and I will move fast, and everything will be okay.

I slip my shoes on and tie them tightly, pulling the gaiters down and securing the small piece of velcro at the back. Pack on, spin around in a quick circle, make sure I'm not leaving anything behind, one trekking pole in each hand, *go.*

The terrain is rougher now, and I hike as quickly as I can across seemingly unending fields of rocks. I hike and hike and hike and hike, legs growing heavy, fully aware that my current pace is unsustainable and yet I can't seem to slow myself down. I turn around every few minutes to check the progression of the dark dark clouds, unable to tell if they are actually moving closer or if my fear is making them appear closer than they really are.

Soon the trail disappears into the rocks entirely, and I hike across a field of sharp talus, thunder booming in the distance, feeling like I'm barely crawling through this mess of stone. I spin in a full circle and can't see a single other person; there is no one out here for miles in any direction, just me and the rocks and the dark, ominous sky.

Oh fuck, I think, as thunder booms again, louder this time. Oh fuck oh fuck.

I am hungry but I do not eat, exhausted but I do not stop, terrified but I do not cry. Not yet. There is no time for crying, no time for anything other than getting down to lower elevation and so I keep going—my fears of getting struck by lightning acting as an adrenaline shot straight to the heart, allowing me to be brave enough to destroy myself, hiking harder than I should, harder than I can sustain, harder than I have maybe ever hiked in my entire life, just absolutely blowing through every ounce of energy to keep my body hurdling forward, away from the storm that's closing in behind me.

Miles pass and I stop only once, just long enough to rip my water bottle from my pack and chug it dry. I can feel that I am sunburnt, that I am shaky with hunger, and I know that I am putting my future self into a deep deficit by not meeting any of these physical needs right now, but I am too scared. Too aware of the thunder, of the fact that there is almost no blue sky left now, of the fact that the final climb is still ahead, the one wherein I need to get myself up to almost 13,000 feet and back down the other side.

I throw myself into it, climbing up up up, choking on my unshed tears. It feels like I am moving backward, like these rocks are quicksand, like I am sinking sinking sinking as a cold wind rips across the mountains, almost blowing me over.

"You just have to get up this final climb," I say out loud. But it feels like I can't, like I have drained myself down past the point of empty, like there is nothing left. Thunder cracks just beyond the next ridge and I scream, throat dry with dehydration, a new spike of fear and adrenaline urging me on, telling me that I will never make it down below the trees in time. I can't out-hike a lightning storm. *Why the fuck did I think that I could out-hike a lightning storm!*

"My name is Nicole Antoinette and I was born to do this," I scream. The words surprise me. I didn't mean to say them, didn't even think them to myself first, but I hear that my voice sounds clear and strong, even against the backdrop of the roaring wind, and so I keep going, keep hiking, keep chanting.

"My name is Nicole Antoinette and I was born to do this. I was born to do this. I was born to do this." I say the words until nothing else exists, until I feel as though I am no longer hiking along the trail but through the words themselves. Up to almost 13,000 feet, cresting the top, trying to flow like water on the descent, not bombing down too hard, protecting my knees, "born to do this, born to do this, born to do this."

There are dark heavy clouds in every direction now, and I rush across the exposed traverse, across boulders and talus, balancing the need to place each foot carefully on the precariously shifting rocks with the equally strong urge to move move move move MOVE.

A few more steps and then I'm off the talus, on the dirt again, throwing myself downhill as fast as I can, running more than hiking as raindrops splash all around me, bright flashes of lightning in my peripheral vision, until the first scraggly tree appears, then another and another until there are finally whole groves of trees and I collapse on the ground underneath them, hiding below the branches as thunder roars and lightning slashes up and over the pass where I was just hiking only moments before. I'm crying now, the sobs I choked back for the past few hours coming free, and I'm shaking with relief, laying on my side in the dirt, cowering in a little ball in my safe forest nook, fully aware that that was the closest call I have ever had.

I lay like this for a while, numbly eating a few bags of fruit snacks, not sure how I will ever be able to stand up again. I just hiked 14.5 miles at high elevation in under 6 hours with thousands and thousands of feet of elevation change, much of it dehydrated and underfed across unstable rock fields in an almost blind panic. I try to slow my breathing, telling myself over and over that I am safe now, I can rest. Minutes pass that feel like hours as the rain turns to hail, big chunks of ice pinging against all the rocks and tree trunks, and I stay tucked up under the branches, head resting on my pack, eyes closed, until eventually the hail slows and stops and I find that I am able to sit up. I rub my eyes, blink a few times, stretch my neck from side to side, trying to orient myself to where I am and what is happening.

I carry my pack down to the nearby creek, sit and filter water amidst the haze of my post-adrenaline zombie fugue state, watch as a few ATVs fly down a nearby dirt road, one man laughing and throwing an empty beer can over his shoulder into the trees as he speeds away. There are some flat spots over in those trees, and my body absolutely needs to be done hiking for the day, has perhaps never needed to be done hiking more than this, but those men and their ATVs make me nervous. Who knows if they could even see me, or if they'll be coming back this way, or if there's any real danger, but when I first started solo hiking back in 2016 I promised myself that I would always follow my own intuition in these situations and right now my intuition is telling me that I can't camp here.

I pull out my map, unable to imagine putting my shoes back on and hiking even five more steps. The terrain does not look promising—I am in a valley between two big climbs right now, which means that if I don't stay here I either need to get all the way up and over the next climb tonight, or else I'll be forced to camp in an exposed place way up high. Why are these my options? I hate all of these options. I just out-hiked a goddamn lightning storm and I need to be done for the day, but now I cannot be done? I put my head in my hands and close my eyes, feeling utterly defeated.

The longer you sit here the darker it's going to get, I think. Which is true. If I'm going to keep hiking I need to keep hiking.

Reluctantly I pull myself together. I pack away my water filter and my snacks. I put my shoes on. I stand up. Another ATV races by, dirt clouds thick in its wake, and even though I know I am making the right call by leaving I suddenly feel so fucking angry. Who are these men to ruin this for me? To make me feel unsafe simply because they exist? I hate these men and I hate hiking and I hate the slippery hail that seems to be covering the ground in every direction.

I can't seem to quell my anger and so I stop trying, I hike with it, I hike in a rage, moving my body up the gently graded switchbacks that are glittering with ice and with shallow puddles of cold rain water, powered by my own dark thoughts. Soon I am in the last of the trees, and I scan the sky for any sign of a second storm, any reason why I shouldn't keep going forward, and even though the clouds still look heavy and full they are no longer a purplish black color and I think (hope) that the danger has passed.

I follow the damp trail out of the trees, into a lush green meadow rimmed with craggy peaks and over-flowing with tiny wildflowers and it is all so astonishingly perfect that I feel as if my heart is breaking. As if I cannot possibly hold the truth of this much beauty, not in my depleted state. My anger melts away, and it feels like what I am seeing in front of me is too achingly good to be real.

I hike through the meadow slowly, barely able to lift my legs after all of today's effort, but the smell of the earth that surrounds me after the deluge of rain, oh my god. This smell is like being reborn. This is what it's like to be in pain and yet to not be suffering. My body is screaming, but I don't know that I've ever felt this way before, physically destroyed but so emotionally at peace, and I marvel at this new experience as afternoon turns to evening and I continue on across the high elevation meadow.

Up and down I go, over each of the damp and grassy climbs, fingers growing numb as the sun drops low over the horizon. The sky is all cotton candy pastels now, soft pink and pale violet, and I know for sure that I am not going to make it down to lower elevation before darkness comes. Every step at this point feels like it is taking all of my willpower, and the 20 miles I have hiked today feel like 30 miles, 40 miles, 100 miles. I see a bright orange tent off to the left about a quarter mile ahead, and I decide that that is where I will stop. I do not know who those people are, nor if they will mind my company, but at this point I do not care. I cannot go any further. Another quarter mile is the absolute best that I can do.

So I gather water at an ice-cold stream just before the tent, and when I get there I am relieved to see that I do in fact know these people, at least a little bit. It's a couple I've leapfrogged with a few times already, and they seem totally fine with me pitching my tent nearby. They try to talk to me as I get set up, but between my increasingly numb hands and the weight of exhaustion I've been carrying for hours I know that I am not good company right now. I mumble my responses, trying to get my tent to stay put in the cold wind up here at 12,000 feet, and as soon as the tent is even somewhat stable I crawl inside and put on every single item of clothing that I have.

Shivering, wearing all of my layers, I unfurl my sleeping bag and shake it out, knowing that the fluffier and more lofted it is the warmer I will be. I shimmy my legs inside of it, letting the rest of the bag bunch up around my waist as I sit in the middle of my small tent, the only spot where I can be upright without my head hitting the top, and I try to talk myself into eating. I have barely eaten anything today, sacrificing my hunger for my lightning fears, but the thought of assembling any kind of meal currently seems like a herculean obstacle that I cannot possibly overcome. I dig around in my food bag, at the mishmash of things I bought at the grocery store, and I pull out the three items I can most easily reach: a bag of bagel chips, a tub of cream cheese, and a two-pack of milk chocolate peanut butter cups. I eat the peanut butter cups first, take a sip of icy water, and then slowing dip the bagel chips into the cream cheese and shove them in my mouth until my fingers are too cold to continue on. Did I eat enough? I try to do calorie math in my head, but like everything else right now that seems entirely impossible.

No more math, I think, tucking my numb hands into my sleeping bag and watching as the last of the sunlight leaves the sky. I did not get struck by lightning today, nothing else matters other than that.

◁ ▷

Day 16

I wake up cozy in my floof sleeping bag, unwilling to move my body and find out the truth about how sore I am from yesterday's hard push. I'm thirsty though, throat dry and achy, so I tentatively reach my arm out from the warm cocoon, grab my water bottle, and chug. As I go to put the cap back on the bottle my shoulder brushes against the side of the tent, and it's then that I notice that all of the condensation on the inside of my tent wall has frozen overnight.

Oh shit! I sit straight up, eyes wide. Last night, after pushing so hard for 20 miles with 10,000 feet of elevation change I was in such a zombie state that I forgot to put my water filter in my sleeping bag. It's a hollow fiber filter, which can crack internally if it freezes, and once that happens the filtration process doesn't work properly. Only there's no way to know for sure whether or not that has actually happened because the filtering mechanism is inside and therefore unable to be seen. This means that I am now in a sort of Schrödinger's cat situation wherein my water filter is either functional or not functional, and the only way I'll know for sure is if I use it and wait to see if I get sick.

Not good, I think. Not good.

I crawl out of my tent, inspecting the thin layer of ice along the outside of the tent walls before I start to pack up in the early dawn light, feeling worried. I'm noticeably dehydrated from yesterday, when all of my needs beyond basic survival got abandoned, and right now I have about three quarters of a liter of water. How long can I make that last? And what will I do when it runs out? I start hiking at 6:45am, unable to stop beating myself up over what feels like such a rookie mistake. I know better! I *always* sleep with my filter when it's cold. Always!

The trail begins to descend shortly out of camp, sunrise glistening off the ice crystals on every rock and leaf and branch and flower, the sight distracting me from my worries for at least a little while. The path is gentle here, wide and mostly clear of rocky obstacles for a few miles before pitching up into the woods, and my footfalls break up the little patches of ice that remain in all the shady areas untouched by the warmth of the morning sun.

I eat some fruit snacks, aware that the big effort at high altitude yesterday has messed with my appetite and that I am nowhere near as hungry as I should be. I eat anyway, hoping that being well-fed will somehow balance out the dehydration, and yet I can't seem to stop obsessing over my dwindling water supply.

Mid-morning comes and I stop to rest at a small lake just off to the side of the trail, right before the start of the steep climb up the first pass of the day. I spread my foam pad out on the ground, do some stretches for my throbbing hip that feels sore and angry from yesterday's talus-filled descending. As I stretch I try to look at my water situation more objectively, to decide on an actual plan. I will soon be out of water and when that happens, what? Am I going to risk using the filter? Am I just going to not drink until Gent meets up with me sometime tomorrow? Neither of these options seem smart, and I take the tiniest sip of water while I try to figure out what to do.

Well, you could keep hiking, I think. Oh. Right. That is the only thing that actually makes any sense, the one thing I know that I must do regardless.

The path away from the lake, up to the top of the nearby pass, is only about half a mile, but for that half mile
it feels as though I am climbing straight up, like the
trail is a never-ending ladder into the sky. My legs do
not like this. Up? What is up, my legs want to know,
and how do we do that again? It is as if my body has
forgotten. Spoiled milk legs: the post-lightning storm
edition.

Eventually I make it to the top where I turn my phone
on in hopes of being able to call Gent, but there is no
service here. There is just the wind and the trail and
the rain clouds, just me and my dehydration and my
spoiled milk legs that are seemingly unable to do what
I need them to do.

I descend for miles after that, not drinking any water,
trying to remain curious and detached about the
mounting headache that is creeping up from the base
of my skull. I stay mad at myself nonstop for hours
while I hike, until finally I begin to cry at just how
exhausting it is to be this mean to myself. I stop walking, still crying, letting my trekking poles fall to the
ground as I wrap my arms around my chest and say,
out loud, "I forgive you, sweetheart. It is okay. You
are allowed to make mistakes."

This becomes my mantra for the next stretch of hiking, this repeated affirmation that I am allowed to

make mistakes, I am allowed to make mistakes, I am allowed to make mistakes, and by the time I reach the next water source, a cold stream of snow melt pouring down the side of the mountain, I feel much less beaten down. I sit there for a while and watch the cascading flow of water, thinking about how strange it is to feel almost painfully thirsty with a pounding dehydration headache while sitting next to such an abundance of water, but I am too afraid to drink it, too afraid of getting sick with giardia. So I finish the couple of sips that are left in my one remaining water bottle, draining it down to empty, put it back into the side pocket of my pack. "Well," I say aloud to no one. "Now what?"

In the absence of any real action steps to take I decide to eat fruit snacks about it, devouring four packs of them in quick succession. Fruit snacks as procrastination; fruit snacks as coping mechanism in the face of total pending dehydration. Eating all that sugar works though, and even if the subsequent energy boost will be short-lived I am not going to waste it while it's here. So I stand up, look at my map, aim toward the river a few miles away, and tell myself that all I need to do is get to that next point. *Just the next right thing*, I think. Just the river. Just a few more miles. Just do that for now.

The day heats up, and I hike on the fumes of my temporary sugar high, headache throbbing incessantly, exhausted legs struggling to get me up and over all the many contours of the earth. I reach the river, sit on the steps of a wooden bridge that will take me to the other side, eat a string cheese, try again to get phone service. But nope, nothing. At some point I'm just going to have to risk getting sick on unfiltered water, right? How long is it reasonable to hike without drinking a single sip?

Across the bridge the trail begins to climb, and I lose myself in the effort of going up for miles and miles. I'm truly scared now, feeling far away from this morning's blasé attitude about how "it'll probably just be fine" because it's now past noon, the sun is beating down, I haven't had water in hours, and it is definitely *not fine.*

The trail takes me past some smaller lakes, each one a teasing oasis that I will not yet let myself drink, terrain getting progressively steeper until eventually it levels out for a stretch on the shores of the largest lake yet. I decide to stop for lunch, to dry my tent that is still bunched up in my pack and soaked from last night's frozen condensation. I lay it out carefully, putting rocks on the corners so it won't blow away, and around the other side of the lake I see an old man fishing by himself. Maybe he has clean water?

I walk carefully around the rocky edges of the lake, getting my shoes wet wherever the shore has disap-peared underneath the sparkling green water, but it's a wasted effort. The fisherman shakes his head when I ask about extra water, barely making eye contact with me, screaming with his body language that he just wants me to leave, so I do.

Back near my tent I position my body into the one small patch of shade I can find, trying to make myself eat something with my dry dry mouth. I'm so hot, and a little dizzy, but I finally have cell reception so I call Gent, lamenting the water filter situation and asking him what he thinks I should do—as if this is a question he can confidently answer for me.

"Maybe your filter isn't broken," he says. "Maybe you can use it and it will be okay?"

Maybe, yeah. But the fear I feel is rooted in the uncertainty of not knowing. If I drink the water, and if my filter isn't working properly, I won't know right away. I'll just be fine until I'm not, and then I'll be sick as hell, and the horror stories I've heard from friends who've experienced giardia in the past make me angry at myself all over again for making this mistake last night.

"I'll figure it out," I tell him. "But I love you. Thanks for talking to me when I am in this state."

Because that's the thing about being the partner of someone who is out on a long-distance hike: it is so hard. The off-trail person is just going about their day, when all of the sudden they get a panicked phone call from the on-trail person who is having some kind of crisis that might not truly be a crisis, but since all your emotions get heightened on trail it makes the stakes for everything feel so incredibly high, and so you've got one person who is dangling off the metaphorical ledge and the other person is just like, "Uh... how do I talk to you right now?" It can be a lot.

A few minutes after I get off the phone with Gent, while I'm packing my things away, a group of three hikers walks down toward the lake, headed the way I came. Oh my god, I think. They probably have a water filter!

I drop everything and sprint up to them, gasp-yelling when I get close enough for them to hear me, begging to use their water filter.

"Uh, sure," one of them says, eyeing me warily, "no problem."

I take it from him, expressing my gratitude over and over again before running down to get the other supplies I'll need. I fill my two liter bladder from the lake, attach his filter to the top of the bladder, and tip it upside down so the clean water can flow into my bottle. But wait, shit, the filter is leaking, and the dirty water is getting into the bottle as well.

Nicole Antoinette

I walk back over to them, handing the guy his filter, and say, "I think there's something wrong with this one. It's leaking. It might be missing the O-ring."

"Oh yeah," he says. "That little white part? It fell out a few days ago."

I stare at him. Why didn't he tell me this? Because now not only do I not have the water I need, I've contaminated my only water bottle with dirty lake water. Damnit!

"You can use my filter if you want," one of the other hikers says. "It definitely works! And I can give you one of my bottles. We need to get going soon though, we're kind of in a hurry."

So I grab the things he holds out for me and I quickly fill up the one liter bottle, no time to drink and filter any more than that, handing the filter back as I put the now full bottle in the side pocket of my pack and turn around to hike out. One liter. I now have one liter of filtered water in a stranger's used water bottle to last me for the rest of the afternoon, all of tonight, and then tomorrow morning until I meet Gent at the highway sometime before lunch. I tell myself that this is fine, that all it means is that I am definitely going to win the imaginary cutthroat competition I have just invented called Dehydration

Rodeo. I am the ultimate thirst cowboy! You cannot defeat me!!

This works for a while—small sip, telling myself that I'm the best ever thirst cowboy, climb steeply for miles, small sip, make cowboy noises, another small sip. At the top of the final climb of the day I lay on the grass in the fierce wind up at 12,500 feet, shirt completely unbuttoned, another small sip of water, astonished to notice that I am still enjoying being out here, somehow, even with my dry throat and my water scarcity fears and this barreling wind that is making it so that I almost cannot hear my own thoughts. Despite all of that I am still having a good time.

There's cell service up here on this grassy plateau on the Continental Divide, and so I stay for a while, letting the wind whip across the exposed skin of my chest, texting Gent and Bugbite, missing them. I swallow the very last of my ibuprofen, hoping it helps calm the headache that has grown from the base of my skull to encapsulate my entire head throughout the day, standing up and hiking out before it kicks in but telling myself that drugs always work and that soon I will feel better.

So I hike on into the wind, rationing the half liter of water I have left as I move across the exposed ridge with my sunburnt skin in the baking heat, no shade.

Nicole Antoinette

I notice the sunburn at the same moment that I notice my butt chafe, which all of the sudden feels as though it is on fire. Who lit my inner ass cheeks on fire in the past 30 seconds, oh my god! I also (even though I have been doing my best to ignore it all day) have some kind of vaginal cyst, or more accurately it is a labia cyst, and for some reason hiking downhill in this precise moment seems to make it feel so much worse. There is an insect bite on the bottom of one of my little toes as well, and a blister on a different toe, and I don't know how none of these things seemed to bother me earlier because right now they are each screaming for attention at the exact same time. So I stop on the side of the trail, no tree cover, completely exposed, shorts and underwear pulled down low as I wet-wipe my ass to soothe the chafe and poke at the labia cyst which is now turning a dark purple color. Great, yep, this is fine. All totally fine.

Shorts back on, I hike, and the trail takes me to the end of the ridge and begins dropping down into a ski area, motionless chairlifts crisscrossing the mountain, all of it feeling strangely creepy in the off-season. I pull out my phone to call Gent again, worried that I am bothering him with my incessant calls and texts today, and I remember that this is the hard thing about being on trail when one's partner is not—you miss them, and you want to talk whenever you have cell service, and so the hiking day moves so slow.

"I still miss you," I say when he picks up.

"What a coincidence," he says. "I'm hiking in from a dirt road crossing with a bunch of water for you right now!"

"You're *what*!" I scream. "Oh my god oh my god okay I'm gonna hike faster love you see you so soon."

I pick up the pace, go go go, and then all of the sudden there he is! The goddamn love of my life, coming toward me in his clean town clothes with big full water bottles on the sides of his pack. We sit down together in the shade and I chug the first bottle he hands me, aware that my stomach is not going to like this sudden flooding but unable to stop. I have been so thirsty for so long now—ever since I started trying to out-run the lightning storm yesterday around noon, over 24 hours and many many miles ago.

"I brought snacks too," he says, pulling grapes and crackers and garlic cheese dip out of his pack. As I eat he gives me two options: "I can fill up your water bottle if you want, and you can keep hiking as planned, and I'll pick you up farther down the trail tomorrow. Or we can go into Salida tonight?"

"Tonight," I say, with no hesitation at all. "Please please take me to town tonight."

We hike together down to the van after that, which is parked on the side of a bumpy dirt road, and when I get there I collapse into the passenger seat, picking up another full bottle of water to chug.

"There's cereal in the back if you want some," Gent says.

And so I eat cereal, and he drives, and then I drink electrolyte water, and he drives, taking us all the way down the mountain to the town of Salida. It feels weird to be back in town so soon; was I really only out on trail for two days since Buena Vista? So much happened in those two days—the lightning and the hail and the men on the ATVs, pushing myself so so hard, the frozen water filter, inadequate food, the dehydration headache and the all-consuming anxiety that comes when one of your basic survival needs is threatened.

We get to the motel, and by the time I climb the stairs to our room I feel like I can barely stand, like all of the adrenaline I've been running on for the past 42 miles has leached out of my body and now there is nothing left.

"I think I need to be managed," I tell Gent, which is our shorthand for when mental capacity is low, a request for the other person to take over and be in charge.

"Take a shower first," he says. So I do.

"Do you want to fill the bathtub when you're done so you can soak your cyst?" he asks. I have told him about the purple bump on my labia and he is convinced that 'purple' means 'ready to pop.'

"Okay," I say. "Yes okay."

I shower, soak in the bathtub, pop the painful cyst.

"Put your legs up the wall for a while," Gent suggests after I've dried off, and so I do that too.

He hands me ibuprofen and I take it. He makes us Annie's white cheddar mac & cheese and I eat it. Afterward he massages my legs with CBD cream, and between his kindness and how much my legs hurt I soon begin to cry. I do not know how to let myself be taken care of like this, not when it's so one-sided. He's the one who had to quit the hike, he's the one who's injured and sad, who decided to stick around in Colorado to wait while I continue doing the thing he so badly wishes he could still be doing too. And now he's hiking out in the middle of nowhere to bring me water, making me dinner, and massaging my legs? It is too much. I cannot receive it.

I cry harder and he soothes me through that too, telling me that he loves me, that I deserve this, that I do not have to do everything alone.

It makes me think about the solo-hike I did four years ago, back in the fall of 2017 on the Arizona Trail when I was terrorized by loneliness almost every day, and I think about how it can be true that one person struggles with both loneliness *and* true partnership. What does that even mean?

◁ ▷

Day 17

It's 7am in the hotel room in Salida and I am spread out like a starfish in my queen size bed.

I am not going to hike today. Not after the emotional whirlwind of Gent getting off trail and then Bugbite getting off trail and then solo hiking 42 miles in two days on three and a half liters of water through a lightning storm with horrendous butt chafe. Nope. No way. He and I need some time together, and we need to plot out the second half of this hike. But first I need to pee.

I'm nervous about getting up, about seeing how severe my hiker hobble is, but it's not actually that bad. I walk from the bed to the bathroom with an almost normal gait! This buoys me immensely, as does the solid night of sleep I just got, and so I am filled with energy as we go first to a coffee shop and order chai lattes and then to a cafe down the street where I eat hash browns and bacon and fruit and buttery rye toast.

Back at the hotel I fall into a deep nap filled with dark dreams—some kind of demon lion is stalking me and I cannot escape it—and when I wake I am disoriented and afraid. Gent and I cuddle, we do laundry, we go to the grocery store and I wander around trying to find anything at all that looks appealing. Something about being so dehydrated seems to have thrown my appetite off again, and the only things I want are cold grapes and pasta with tomato sauce, which I buy in addition to the random foods I've thrown into the cart for this next section of the hike.

Back at the hotel again, soaking in an epsom salt bath, I eat handfuls of grapes while the steamy air helps to soothe the cough that has steadily been getting worse over the past week, the cough I made the mistake of googling last night even though I know better than to google my symptoms. "Coughing" and "high elevation" do not produce comforting search results, but I decide that eating grapes will fix it, that eating grapes will maybe fix everything—my lack of appetite, my fiery butt chafe, my hiker ego that tells me I shouldn't be taking a rest day today, that I should be hiking harder and faster, that if I were truly strong I'd be much farther down the trail by now.

Just keep eating these grapes, I tell myself. The grapes will save us all.

The rest of the day passes quickly: organizing my resupply, massaging my sore muscles, stretching and sex and pasta marinara eaten in bed while bundled up with all the blankets. I try not to think about the morning, when I will need to leave the comfort of my partner and our motel cocoon, when I will begin this hike all over again.

260 miles down, 231 to go. And in those 231 miles, what?

◁ ▷

Day 18

I sleep for 8 hours, waking up to sex and cereal and a hot hot shower. My body feels so good today—strong, powerful, alive.

We go back to the same cafe for breakfast before driving up into the mountains. The air is smoky, not from any nearby fires but from the many that are raging out in Oregon and Idaho. It's mostly just bad out in the distance though, a lack of long-range visibility, and once we park and step out of the van the air smells fresh enough.

Gent's achilles is feeling okay this morning, so he hikes out with me for about a mile and a half before turning around. Alone again, I make my way up into the hot, dry hills, no water for miles, stepping carefully over all the rocks and jumping out of the way of the bikes that are back now that I'm nearing the end of the Collegiate West Loop (where they are not allowed) and rejoining the main Colorado Trail.

The route for a while is mostly ridge walking, trail contouring around the sides of the mountains. I move entirely at my own pace, slow, comfortable, taking as many breaks as I want. There is no one else to negotiate with, no other feelings to take into consideration other than my own—the best part of solo hiking.

Seven miles in, snack break. Another few miles, water break. I've vowed to take such sweet care of myself in this section, eating enough, drinking enough, resting often, tending to my butt chafe. Now that I've borrowed Gent's water filter and I'm not dehydrated or hustling out of lightning storms above tree line I can relax, try not to wind up as utterly fucked as I was in the last section.

The miles pass slowly and the trail feels quiet all day, a few bikers but no hikers who are going my same direction. Where is everybody? Ah well, I enjoy my own company. Hiking alone for 10+ hours a day is unlike anything else I have ever done. It strengthens my friendship with myself, which is the foundation of my relationship with my sobriety, with my writing, with god, with everything.

10 miles in and I lay on the ground, pulling my knees to my chest, stretching my glutes and my hamstrings, staring up at the wispy clouds in the bright blue sky, feeling grateful that my body is strong and that I was brave enough to keep going after both of my hiking partners had to quit. It would have been so easy for me to quit as well, to use the abrupt change in plans as a reason to give up, but I do not want to give up. I want to hike on my own two legs all the way to Durango.

Afternoon comes, and it is all thick forests and cold drizzle, abandoned dirt roads and herds of cows and squelchy mud, followed by a miles-long descent that is mostly just a steep mess of rocks and slippery gravel. I trip a few times, the rocks sliding out from under my feet, and it's right around then that the quiet and the solitude stops feeling so delightful. I am bored of my own thoughts, bored of thinking in general, so I turn on an audiobook and promise myself that when

I don't want to hike anymore I can stop for the night and be done.

The trail soon flattens out a bit, just a narrow strip of dirt cutting through the otherwise dense forest, and just before 7pm, after hiking 19.5 miles, I find a small flat spot nestled in the trees, just big enough for my tent. There are so many more options for where to camp when you are alone, when you can squeeze your little one-person tent into any random flat spot, and I love this, love how being alone makes me nimble. But it also makes me lonely, and as I pitch my tent I remember that the end of the day is always when I most crave company out here. I haven't camped entirely alone since 2018, so of course it is going to feel strange again at first. But that will pass. We can get used to absolutely anything if only we give ourselves the chance.

I crawl into my tent and begin pulling things out of my food bag. I eat a bagel with cream cheese, half a package of mint Milano cookies, a jumbo Kit-Kat bar. I blow up my sleeping pad, watch the sun as it sets through the trees, let the loneliness wash over me.

"You're fine," I tell myself. "You're fine and you're safe. Just climb into your squish sleeping bag and read for a while. You will sleep. Tomorrow will come. Everything is going to be okay."

◁ ▷

Day 19

I had a hard time falling asleep last night, spooked by the creaking trees and nocturnal animal noises. Being alone in the darkness of the woods can feel either freeing or terrifying, depending on my mood. It'll get better though. I'll get used to this again.

After I finally fell asleep I was soon woken up again, the sounds of rain pouring down through the leafy branches and pelting against the walls of my tent. I stayed dry and warm though, tucked up tight in a little ball inside my sleeping bag, and when morning comes I find that I am still in this ball, trying to coax myself to get up.

Eventually I do, peering out into the misty morning, tent soaked from last night's rain, a melancholy mood settling into my chest. I pack up, eat a bar, take a few sips of my chocolate protein shake, and begin to hike. The trail is still a mess of rocks, and everything from my knees down is feeling the impact of that, feeling it badly. From the knees up my body seems fine, great, maybe even a little super-human, but from the knees down? Ugh.

The rain starts and stops all morning, clouds heavy, the hood of my rain jacket pulled tight around my face, nowhere to stop and dry out my sopping wet tent. I walk through the woods, morale low, each up-hill feeling so much more efforty than I expect, as if the trail is covered in waist-deep molasses. I check the map again and again—Gent is meeting me at a re-mote trailhead for lunch, about 8 miles into my day, and I keep telling myself that all I need to do is make it there. Just make it there. But these 8 miles feel like 12. Like 15. Like an endless expanse of ground that I will never be able to cover, and when I finally get up and over the climb to that trailhead and see him waiting for me I feel a little astonished that I actually made it here, that I wasn't somehow walking back-ward all along.

The van is parked about a half mile away, its low clearance and front-wheel drive unable to make it up the remainder of the rough road, and I see that Gent has hauled a foldable chair and lots of snacks up here for me, earning his trail name again and again. We hide from the rain together, tucked under the wide, low branches of a sprawling tree. It's so good to have him here, but it's hard too—it makes me wish we were still doing this hike together the way we planned.

The wind whips through our little clearing, rain pelting down harder, and I mindlessly eat grapes and

Goldfish as I wait for the sky to clear. I drink orange juice, eat a bagel with cream cheese, pack out a second bagel for later because bagels are apparently all that I really want to eat now?

75 minutes of huddling later and it's time for me to hike on, audiobook playing, hands balled up inside my fleece mittens, cold down to my bones. The morale boost from seeing Gent wears off quickly, especially as the rain returns and a big group of dirt bikers run me right off the trail. It's one of those days where everything is technically fine, but I'm just kind of over it. Hiking all day is great until it's not, and today is one of the nots.

But it'll pass, it always does, and knowing that all feelings come and go on a hike like this helps me to not over-attach to any of the ones I don't like. So yes I feel kind of shitty, but I am not panicking about that and this means that at least I am not making it worse for myself. Sometimes that is the win: simply not making yourself feel worse by beating yourself up over feeling bad in the first place.

I hike all afternoon in my haze of not-good-mood, taking my rain coat on and off and on and off each time the weather changes, contorting my body into the dense branches of a tree to give myself shelter during a brief but violent hailstorm. My bad mood persists, but I try to find pleasure in a few small delights, such as the return of the brightly colored mushrooms that are once again popping up all over the forest floor. I love all these mushrooms! I stop to get a closer look, bending down so my face is only a few inches from their fire engine red caps, careful not to touch what I believe to be poisonous fungi. *These are just for looking*, I remind myself. *Don't touch.*

I find a spot near the mushrooms, a clear section of ground where I can spread out my little foam butt pad and sit for a while. I eat string cheese and chips and fruit snacks and nuts, surprised by how hungry I am. Finally! Oh my god. I eat more chips. I eat more cheese. I eat some chocolate. I eat and eat and eat.

Miles later I reach a water source, a creek that has been reduced to just a small trickle, but if I am patient I can easily gather what I need. I crouch there and slowly fill my water bladder, surprised by how dry today has been in terms of water sources. When I'm done filtering, when both of my bottles are full, I decide to stay a little longer, sipping water and eating chips, taking advantage of the small amount of sun that finally peeks out from behind the dark clouds, using it to dry my tent.

A few miles later I make camp; it's only 5:50pm but in the few miles between the water source and here the tendon above my right ankle has gotten spitting mad, probably from all the rocky terrain these past few days, and it hurts enough that I know I need to rest. I'm torn though, because I really don't like stopping this early when I am alone, when there's no one else to talk to for all the hours between 6pm and bedtime.

At first I wonder what I will do with all this time, and then I decide that I will use this time to eat. How much of my food can I eat tonight without fucking over Tomorrow Me? I care about Tomorrow Me, I do not want her to be starving, but Current Me is starving now and, well. I spread the entire contents of my food bag on the floor of my tent, separating out the things I am absolutely not allowed to eat tonight. The bare minimum I will need for tomorrow before I meet up with Gent again at the end of the day. Everything else is fair game, I tell myself, and then I go to work on it.

First I rehydrate a packet of white cheddar instant mashed potatoes in my cold-soaking jar, eating cookies while I wait. When the potatoes are ready I cover them in those crispy fried onions, the kind I usually only buy to use as topping for green bean casserole, and oh my god have I just discovered the meaning of life? This meal is so good. So so good, and I spoon it into my mouth gratefully. Grateful for the food, grateful to finally be so hungry, to feel like my body is working the way it is supposed to work.

This is enough, I realize. A dry tent, a warm sleeping bag, deliciously weird dinner, a pile of snacks to continue eating and the contentment of having moved myself another 22 miles closer to my goal.

That is more than enough for now.

◁ ▷

Day 20

The storm starts just before 1am, wind howling like a tortured animal, rain making a loud tat-tat-tat against my tent. It's so intense that I can't fall back asleep for hours, and dawn comes much too quickly.

I peer out from my sleeping bag at 6am, damp air immediately blasting my face and nope, no way, back into the sleeping bag cocoon, back to sleep. What finally gets me up about an hour later is that I have to poop, badly. The world's most effective alarm clock. I shimmy out of my sleeping bag, grab my puffy coat, put my shoes on, climb out of the tent. I've got my toilet paper bag in one hand and my trowel in the other, and I walk out into the damp woods to find a good spot to dig my hole. It's so cold though, and I'm clumsy as I try to dig the hole with my numb hands, almost not getting it dug deep enough in time. But I make it, I do not shit myself, and this is a (not so) small victory on which I can now build my entire mood for the day.

It's 7:30am when I finally get my stuff all packed, and as I hike out I can tell right away that my ankle tendon feels noticeably better. Still, I carefully watch each step of the rocky early morning terrain until eventually the rocks end and the trail merges with a series of well-graded dirt roads instead. I am so relieved! You mean I no longer need to micromanage every single foot placement? You mean I can just... walk?

And so I do, 3 miles, 5 miles, 8 miles.

I meet a few new people throughout the morning and we leapfrog for hours, keeping each other company on the long dirt roads that take us through ranching land where the threat of stepping into piles of fresh cow shit greets us around every bend. The route makes this what I call a "connector day", wherein you don't see any sweeping views and are instead just doing the work of connecting your footpath between one lovely place and another. I'm out of the Collegiates now, but not yet into the San Juans, and so I walk along dirt roads for 10 miles, 15 miles, 18 miles, listening to audiobooks and making mental gratitude lists and fantasizing about town food. I sing loudly in my off-key voice, serenading each herd of cows that I pass, moving more quickly than I usually would because of the flatter, rock-free terrain.

There are a few gentle climbs, then a few short steep climbs, then a rusted gate that I cannot open and need to slide underneath on my belly to get to the other side. I eat cold-soaked cous cous and handfuls of fried onions for lunch, sitting under a tree with two of the guys I've met today, whose trail names are Milkshake and EFT.

"Eating For Two," he says, explaining the acronym. "I packed way too much food at the beginning, enough for at least two hikers."

"And Milkshake is short for Baby Milkshake," says the other guy. "I'm a neonatal nurse; I spend a lot of time mixing up formula and bottle-feeding tiny babies."

I finish my cous cous, drink water with an electrolyte tablet and a few squirts of fruit punch mixed in, using it to swallow a dose of ibuprofen. My ankle tendon is angry again (the less varied terrain of all the dirt roads, maybe?) and I want to keep hiking at a good pace so that I can meet Gent at our planned camp spot before it gets too late.

I hike out alone, feeling it the moment the painkillers kick in, crossing the 300-mile mark and using

the absence of pain as a chance to turn on my upbeat playlist and fly. By 4pm I've already gone over
20 miles, and there's Gent! He's parked at the dirt
road intersection we found on the map, surrounded
by ground that is flat enough for our tents, a little
backcountry slumber party.

I pitch my tent as soon as I get there, so that last night's
dampness can dry in the late afternoon sun, and then
I collapse on the ground. I make a feeble attempt to
stretch, but what I really want is a leg massage. Some
good strong pressure to encourage my ankle tendon
to get its shit together. Gent does this for me, and
then we each make our own pots of fettuccine alfredo,
me using my cook kit that's stored in the van. We eat
this while sitting crosslegged on the ground together,
followed by a bagged salad that he brought for us, the
crisp lettuce tasting so good after so many days of
processed food.

I'm quiet as we finish our dinner, feeling exhausted
and also struggling to parse through my reaction to
Gent's continued kindness, the way he keeps showing
up and giving to me with his whole heart. How will I
ever repay him for this? And why do I feel like kindness
is transactional, that "repayment" is even needed?

I think about this as I zip myself into my sleeping bag,
about love and reciprocity and unconditional support.

I thought I was coming out here to hike with two of my beloved people, to experience an adventure from inside our tiny roving community. And then they both had to quit and I thought that maybe I was out here to spend time alone with myself, because I owed it to myself to continue on even if it meant doing so alone.

But now, what? Am I out here to allow myself to be supported? Is the real thing that I owe to myself not just the chance to keep going on my own but to keep going with such full-hearted support beside me the entire way?

I suppose I have 170 miles left to find out.

◁ ▷

Day 21

Coyotes yip and howl all throughout the night, the sound waking me and then mixing into a series of strange kaleidoscopic dreams.

I can't believe how cold it got last night, and this morning I keep my sleeping bag huddled around my legs and waist as I eat a bagel smothered in cream cheese and look at the map to see what's ahead for today. Lots of climbing, it looks like. But lots of water too. Frequent water means a lighter pack, and this boosts my morale. I've been feeling sad since I woke up, sad that each time I get to see Gent also means hiking away from him again and again. Maybe he should meet up with me less often? Would that make it better or worse?

We hike out together in the cold and biting morning air, me wearing my mittens and my rain coat and my buff up around my face. After two miles Gent stops to turn around, stands next to a metal gate and watches me until we are both just tiny specks in each other's distant landscape.

Alone, I move across the dirt roads for miles and miles, finally climbing up into a grove of aspens, sighing in relief at once again being surrounded by these trees that I adore. A few more miles, out of the wooded area, trail circling a large pond where a bull moose drinks and eyes me warily. The closer I get the more still he becomes, until I'm directly across from him on the other side of the pond and he takes off running up a hill and into the meadow beyond.

I check my map—this spot is where Milkshake and EFT said they were going to camp last night, which means they've got to be decently far ahead of me by now. I try to sift through how I feel about this, about my craving to spend time with other hikers and the disjointed social experience that the Colorado Trail has been for me so far. During the first week it felt like I was meeting multiple new folks each day, but now? There are hardly any other hikers. Where did everybody go?

I follow the trail as it winds through the damp green valley along the Cochetopa Creek, walking down to the water's edge whenever I need to refill my bottle. I feel good today, dirty and alive and perfectly tiny as I move in the shadows of all the surrounding, towering peaks.

14 miles in and I stop for a lunch break, the first time I've properly sat down all day. I eat chocolate covered pretzels and fruit snacks and chips and a small bag of trail mix. I take my shoes off, try to relax, try to make myself sit here longer but I can't. I'm restless. A hiker named Kevin comes by, looks at me with his head tilted, says he recognizes me from Instagram. I've been micro-blogging from the trail, sharing stories and photos along the way, and he's been reading them each time he goes into town.

"I've been hiking 30-ish miles a day," he says. "Have you seen three younger dudes pass by? They are trying to do a 35 today."

I shake my head, packing up my things soon after he wanders off, and as I put my shoes on I realize

that this is why I've been alone so much out here—
everyone I do meet has said they are either doing
about 14 miles a day or 30+ miles a day and I am
somewhere in the middle, leaving me consistently on
my own. I think about this as I start to hike into the
early afternoon, about what it would feel like to be
able to hike more than 30 miles a day, every day.
Eventually those three guys that Kevin mentioned
come storming up the trail, and I step aside to let
them pass. They are in front of me for a too-short
moment and then they are gone, their quick legs
carrying them up and away like an illusion, like they
were never here at all.

Hours pass with very few breaks, and I get lost in the
flow of it all, the wet creek crossings, the thick vege-
tation that brushes against my legs as I hike and hike
and hike and hike.

It's only 3:30 when I reach my planned camp spot, 21
miles done and I still feel like I'm deep in the hiking
flow, so why not push it and see how far I can go.
Sometimes it feels good to push. To really try. To dig
in and see what's possible. I look at my map, I look
up at the pass in front of me, thousands of feet above.
Why not, I think.

I feel good for another mile and then my legs start
to grow heavy, ankle tendon throbbing, feet suddenly

so sore and sensitive that every step feels like there are hot coals in my shoes. The total body breakdown comes on shockingly fast, but I'm committed now, already on the part of the climb where there are no flat spots to stop. There is only forward and up, there is the pass and the fact that I must now get to the other side of it before the soft grey clouds above me turn menacing.

I move one step at a time, which is of course the way I always move because all we can ever do is go one step at a time, but right now it *feels* like one step at a time because I am so acutely aware of all the little pains in my body. I marvel at this, at how my body can go from feeling great to feeling like utter trash in such quick succession. I slow down as much as I need to, climbing up and up and up, relieved when I finally reach the top. I shove a bar in my mouth, holding my hat in place against the rough wind, barely getting my jacket on in time before the first raindrops start to fall.

The rain soon turns to hail, and I hike along the exposed trail that contours the inner rim of these mountains. There is absolutely nowhere to hide should the hail be followed by lightning, so I try not to think about that, try to enjoy the sight and sound of each little ice chunk as it pings against the rocks and dirt all around me.

It's okay, I tell myself, it's just a little hail. Keep going. You're fine. Gradual and relentless forward progress. My body seems to be disintegrating though, my inflamed tendon and some stabbing sensation in my right shin and something deep and achy in my left hip. Didn't I feel strong this morning, and even this afternoon? Didn't I feel strong just a little while ago, at the bottom of this pass? What is happening to me right now?

One more saddle to go, up and over, and then I descend a little ways into a small grove of bushes with a few spindly trees where the ground is not quite flat but might be flat enough. Just flat enough, just sheltered enough. Should I try to get to even lower ground? Probably. But my body will not let me. My body is absolutely *done.*

I check the time as I immediately start to pitch my tent. The rain and hail have stopped, but I know that once I sit down I will have a very hard time getting back up, so all of the camp chores must be done and they must be done now. It's only 5:20pm though—somehow I hiked 25 miles and, wait, did I seriously only take 45 minutes of proper breaks today? No wonder I feel like this.

Tent pitched, I climb inside and devour everything in my food bag that I don't absolutely positively definitely need for tomorrow—my new evening routine. I eat cous

cous and cheese and cookies and chips and chocolate, so much chocolate, licking my dirty fingers clean when I'm done. It's surprisingly cold this evening, so after my little feeding frenzy I put on all of my warm clothes, everything I've got, and I lay down in my tent with my back against the good hard earth, bundled up in my sleeping bag but not yet laying on my inflatable pad, letting my back flatten out on the ground, feeling utterly content. All of my needs are met in this moment—I am well-fed and warm and still—and I am feeling that soft and exquisite peace that only comes when I've pushed myself hard enough for long enough that all of my bullshit fades away and I am left with nothing but a deep internal quiet, that richly empty sound of having nothing else to do, of knowing that where I am in this moment is exactly right.

◁ ▷

Day 22

Holy fuck I am sore. It's almost as if hiking 25 miles with just 45 minutes of breaks is a bad idea or something?

I pull my sleeping bag up over my face, absolutely dreading even the thought of getting up. It's only 16 miles to the highway into town today, but as I stare at the map on my phone I see that what awaits me in those 16 miles is 8,000 feet of elevation change.

How, I think. Just... how.

I do not want to move, not even a little bit, but I know that Gent will be waiting for me at the highway and that the miles between us are not going to hike themselves. Staying here, scowling at the map all morning and stubbornly refusing to move will not do a single thing to make the upcoming terrain any easier, and so eventually I take a deep breath, tell myself out loud that I am brave and tough, and then I reach behind me to deflate my sleeping pad— the woosh of air coming out of its valve acting like a "no turning back now" nudge that makes me finally sit up, change my clothes, pack my things, and go.

Right away it's steep, trail going straight up, straight down, 20+ mph winds in which my hat flies off my head once, twice, a third time, me running around after it until I finally get smart enough to take it off and shove it in my pack instead.

My body drags all morning; I'm tired from yesterday's bigger mileage, my legs are not fully cooperating, that damn tendon above my right ankle protests loudly on all the descents. It's beautiful here though, green and wide open, bright blue sky, and once I can change my mindset to remember that the challenges aren't personal, that the trail isn't steep *at* me, I feel better. The trail is just the trail; what a privilege to walk along it.

I crest one pass, two passes, three, up and over again and again. There was another hiker with me for a little while this morning but he is long gone now, his fast legs taking him over the first pass of the day in the same amount of time it took me to get even halfway up. So now I am alone again, and all of the sudden I feel like I am going to faint, the hills turning into wavy green shapes in front of my eyes. Low blood sugar, maybe? The ghosts of all the calories I couldn't eat for the first half of the trail when I was caught in perpetual nausea, coming back to haunt me?

I sit on the ground and rest my head between my knees, taking slow, steady breaths. I drink some water, take more deep breaths, but the feeling does not pass. Food, I think, I need food. So I stay there in the dirt and I shovel handfuls of Goldfish and chocolate pretzels into my mouth and almost immediately the hills stop swaying in front of my face. Oh! Chocolate is the secret, I realize. Chocolate is how I will climb these climbs today.

So I dig into my food bag, scrounging for all the remaining chocolate. There are two small bars of milk chocolate and another ziplock bag of chocolate pretzels, and I shove all of them into my fanny pack so that they are easy to reach. I hike a little, eat some chocolate, hike a little more, eat more chocolate—and it's in this way that I finally reach the high point of today's terrain where I stop and rest and trace the trail with my eyes as it winds around and around into the distance, a full view of the San Juan mountains spread out in front of me—majestic and intimidating.

There is one tiny bar of cell service here, and I lose myself in the internet and the little dings and bings of each text message I've received since I last had service a few days ago. And those texts are great, but they are not the main reason I've been checking for service every few hours since yesterday afternoon. It's my beloved friend Kate, a professional track athlete who raced in a prestigious meet yesterday, and I am dying to watch it and see how she did. Is the video saved online anywhere? I google "2021 Prefontaine Classic women's 800m race" and boom, it pops right up and I press play on the two-minute video, screaming and cheering alone on this mountain ridge as Kate fights her way into a second place finish.

Lit up by the toughness and speed and determination of my friend, I blow through the next few miles, music blasting, high on the endorphins of having now made it hundreds of miles on my own two feet. I move across the wide expanse of Snow Mesa, eating the final bites of my chocolate as I drop down and begin the steep descent toward the trailhead, my pace coming to an almost grinding halt as the downhill movement sends wave after wave of fiery pain through my ankle tendon.

Gent is with me now, having hiked out to keep me company for these final few miles as I inch down toward the road, and I ask him for reassurance over and over again.

"This will be fine, right? My tendon will heal? Maybe I need new shoes? Will it be okay? Please tell me it's going to be okay."

This relentless need for external reassurance is one of the ways my anxiety disorder manifests, and even though I've been diligently taking my Lexapro each day on trail I still find that the obsessive worry creeps up whenever I am in physical pain. Ankle tendon: 1, Lexapro: 0.

"Yes," Gent says, "I promise it will be fine."

We finally cross the road at the base of the descent, my van parked in the lot on the other side. There's a cold bottle of orange juice waiting for me on the passenger seat, my favorite trail treat. I drink it greedily as we drive down to Lake City, a small town that has everything I need: hot shower, crispy fries, grocery store, laundry machine, all the places to do the usual chores plus an old fashioned ice cream shop where I order big scoops of mint chocolate chip in a waffle cone and Gent gets his first ever root-beer float.

Back in our motel room that night I pick at the enormous callous on my heel, pretty sure that there's some kind of blister deep down underneath the hardened skin.

"I've got some sandpaper in the van," Gent says. "Want me to file it down?"

At first I think he is joking, but apparently he is not.

"Uh, sure?" I say. "If you want?"

And so we end the day with my foot in his lap as he gently buffs the bulbous callous down into something that will hopefully fit better inside my shoe, and I think again about the phrase "unconditional love" — because if sandpapering someone else's gross heel callous in a small motel room in the middle of nowhere doesn't count as unconditional love then I truly do not know what does.

◁ ▷

Day 23

Someone in the motel room next to ours snores loudly all night long, and so even though I am warm and comfortable in here I spend most of the night awake, turning up the volume on my white noise app, fantasizing about hexing this stranger who gets to sleep soundly at the expense of every other person within hearing distance.

I climb from my bed into Gent's bed in the early dawn hours, daylight only just starting to shine through the gaps in the motel curtains, and I cuddle up against him as he talks to me about his sadness, about how he feels like he failed this hike, about how much he wishes he were still doing it with me the way that we had planned.

Balancing his sadness with the fact that I am so deeply immersed in the details and excitement and logistics and big emotions of the remainder of my own hike feels disorienting—it's like I can be there for him or I can be there for myself but doing both at the same time is almost more than I have the capacity to handle right now. I don't like that this is true, that I don't seem able to hold the complexity of both of our feelings with the same amount of care and grace, and yet it's how I feel. I try though. I listen to him and I hold him and each time my mind launches forward into all that remains ahead of me I gently reel it back, focus on Gent, try to stay present for him.

Eventually we get up, eat greasy buttered bagels at the coffee shop, get my resupply box from the post office, do laundry. My plan for the day is to take it easy this morning, leave Lake City and get on trail after 2pm, hike about 10 miles, give my ankle tendon a bit of a break, not overdo it. But all of the chores are done, we check out of our little cabin at noon, there's nothing left to do in town, and I'm restless.

So Gent drives me back up to the pass, and by 12:45pm I'm hiking slowly up the dirt road into the San Juan mountains with Milkshake, who got dropped off by a trail angel along with a bunch of other hikers right after we pulled into the trailhead parking lot. It's nice to have company for an hour or so, but I can tell that he wants to hike faster than me, that I'm slowing him down, and so I encourage him to go on without me.

"I'm sure I'll see you later in this section," I say. "I won't be too far behind!"

But maybe that's not true? Maybe I'll never catch him. I really don't like trying to keep pace with faster hikers (even though I do love having someone to talk to), and so when I meet someone whose company I enjoy it's always a battle in my mind between which thing I want more: companionship or the ease of moving at my own pace. How hard am I willing to push myself so that I don't have to be alone? Today's answer is: not very hard.

So Milkshake hikes out ahead, quickly disappearing into the distance as the road turns to thin rocky trail, winding across a wide and entirely exposed plateau, storm clouds gathering about a half mile behind me.

I hike slowly, picking my way amongst the rocks, a strong headwind pushing into my body as I sort through my heartbroken feelings for Gent, knowing he wants to be out here so badly, struggling with the fact that his injury is a problem I can't swoop in and solve. I hike and hike, feeling weighed down by both my full pack and my heavy emotions, talking myself in circles about why I'm still out here—should I have quit too?

It takes me three hours to reach the first water source, right near where I had planned to camp, but it's so early. If I stop now, what? I'll just be sad and lonely in my tent for many many hours, an entirely unappealing prospect.

I find Milkshake taking a break by the water. EFT, our other new friend, is apparently a few miles ahead, and the two of them are planning to hike all the way up and over the trail's high point tonight.

Nicole Antoinette

Well that's ambitious, I think as I watch Milkshake leave. An almost 19 mile day with absurdly high eleva-tion climbs starting as late as we did this afternoon? I was supposed to go easy today. I was supposed to give my angry little tendon a break. I rotate my ankle out in front of me a few times and it feels okay. So maybe it's fine?

It's 4pm now, and I once again try to imagine camping by myself just up ahead where I had planned, but nope, no, I do not want to do that. Fuck it—if Milkshake and EFT can make it up and over the high point tonight then so can I.

I quickly filter some water, shove a peanut butter and jelly sandwich in my mouth, grab my pack, and head upward above tree line. The wind is fierce up here as I hike across exposed meadows under a tempestuous sky, and I hold onto my hat so it doesn't blow away. I motivate myself with fruit snacks, with good music, with chocolate, with out loud pep talks about how I am a badass bitch, and it is in this way that I hike myself up up up, higher and higher in the early evening sun, heart pounding as I make it across a spicy little rock scramble for which I need both hands.

Over the top of the scramble I find Milkshake and EFT sitting near the cliff's edge, laughing and taking photos of the almost otherworldly view, jagged mountains

182

and crystalline blue lakes that stretch out before us, one after the other into what feels like an infinity of beauty.

It's about two miles from here to the high point. We all set off together, EFT in the front, Milkshake close behind him, me doing my best to keep up now that I've committed to this, to coming up here, which also means I've committed to getting as far as I can down the other side of the mountain before dark, not wanting to camp in this wild wind above 13,000 feet.

Our group stays together on the flats and strings out whenever the trail pitches upward, me watching their seemingly motorized legs churn just as fast on the climbs as on the flatter terrain. How, I wonder, watching them pull out ahead of me on each ascent. How do they *do* that?

We make it to the top though, all of us together, and we take turns dancing around the signpost that marks the Colorado Trail's high point: 13,271 feet.

"Down?" EFT asks.

"Down," I say back, looking at the clock (7pm) and at how the bright egg yolk sun has already fallen so low in the sky.

And so down we go, slipping and sliding for miles on the loose gravel as we make our way into the deep green valley, me finally able to keep pace with them, but only just. (It's not a thru-hike until you eventually find yourself racing sunset in the freezing wind with a couple of kindly 20-something dude bros, right?)

Down down down we hike, sun dropping away, calling it quits at the first (sort of) flat spot we see below us, a spot that is mostly sloped but good enough. I pick my way down the steep hillside to reach this flat-ish area, working quickly to pitch my shelter against the backdrop of the bruised purple sky, temperature plummeting, putting on every layer of clothing I've got and hiding in my tent to try and get warm while the guys sit in front of their own tents, a little ways off, talking and cooking. How they have any energy left is beyond me. Cooking? I cannot imagine. And so I sit in my sleeping bag, cocooned in my own fatigue, the last dregs of adrenaline from these 19 intense miles seeping out of my body, leaving me spent.

I feel calm though, proud of having made it all the way here to this spot below the high point once I decided that that's what I wanted to do today. I pull my buff over my ears, cinch the hood of my puffy jacket tighter around my head, keeping in as much warmth as I can. I eat a string cheese, a dried fruit bar, and an entire bag of chocolate chip cookies for dinner, listening to the soft sounds of chatter with occasional bursts of laughter from outside my tent, my whole body tingling with soreness and yet awash in a sensation of complete and total satisfaction.

◁ ▷

Day 24

The ground under my tent turns out to be much more sloped than I initially thought—one of the risks of pitching one's tent when it is mostly dark—and so sleep eludes me for the majority of the night.

In the morning I'm exhausted, clumsy, and completely unprepared for the steep two miles out of camp. There is no warm-up, no easing in. There is only the moment when I shoulder my pack and then the moment immediately afterward when I need to coax my legs into doing something that they very much seem incapable of doing.

Has hiking always been this hard? How have I hiked almost 400 miles on these legs that now seem to want to do nothing other than stay completely still? I don't know if it's that I'm sore, that I hardly slept, that the shock of going from laying down to hiking steeply uphill is too much or what, but it takes me over an hour to move myself two miles and in that hour I begin to spiral into existential crisis. How is this what I am doing with my life? Which past mistakes led me here? What even is the purpose of a human life? Why can't I want something else? Who would ever, ever want to strap all their stuff to their back and haul their body up a sharply angled pass first thing in the morning for no reason? What the actual fuck is wrong with me for choosing this?

I hike up and up, trapped in the incessant internal hellstorm of what I've now dubbed The Existential Crisis Climb: a climb so jarring that it makes you question literally everything about who you are and what and why.

But my body warms up eventually, and soon the terrain flattens out, taking the power of my existential crisis right along with it. The rest of the morning after that is perfect blue skies, not a single cloud to be seen, hiking and eating one pack of fruit snacks after another. Thank goodness for past me who packed an almost obscene abundance of fruit snacks for this section!

I leapfrog with other hikers as we each take our various mid-morning breaks, some folks that I've met before and others who are new to me, who are only out for this weekend. I pass these folks, they pass me, cows meandering around us along a trail that somehow manages to be both rocky and lush at the same time.

For hours I climb and descend, climb and descend, always surrounded on all sides by the mountains. I wish I could adequately describe how this feels, to be one lone person walking at 2.5 mph through a mountain range, how beautifully small it makes you feel, the reminder of how fleeting and precious your lifespan is compared to these monoliths of stone. *This is actually a wonderful thing to be doing with your life*, I tell myself, remembering my earlier crisis.

The hours pass. The miles pass. I take breaks, eat chocolate covered pretzels, lay in the grass, chug water from ice cold streams, talk to my new friends when I see them. I did about 9 more miles than planned yesterday, which means that I can take today at a much more leisurely pace, no need to hike too far, not with a plan already in place for Gent to meet me at the highway late tomorrow afternoon. And yet every time I think about stopping for the day I find a reason to keep going instead—either the spot is too exposed, or not flat enough, or it's too early. And besides, I feel good, right? I can keep hiking.

But by 3pm I begin to wilt, no shade anywhere, the allure of hour upon hour in the mountains wearing thin. It's like the cumulative effect of no sleep plus an entire day spent hiking in the blazing sun high above tree line crashes into me all at once, and I stand on the side of the trail feeling confused about what time it is and how long it's been since I've seen another person, knowing that Milkshake and EFT passed me many hours ago.

"Just three more big climbs," I say to myself, looking down at the map to check how far I'll need to go if I want to make it below tree line for the night. I could camp near here, but I've already come this far, might as well keep going, right? Ensure I'll have a safer night at lower elevation? It's just 8 more miles. I can do 8 more miles.

The first climb is fine, I lose myself in the effort while Taylor Swift blasts in my ears. The second climb is less fine, long and lonely and relentlessly windy, and I stop two different times to curl into a little ball on the ground, head tucked up into my arms, not sure if I am hugging myself or shielding myself from the wind or what I even need anymore. I make myself drink water. I make myself eat an entire jar of cold-soaked parmesan cous cous. There, I think. Now I can finish this second climb. So I do, still with absolutely no shade, still being pummeled by the wind, still aware that I could theoretically stop anywhere, pitch my tent, be done for the day—so what's driving me? It's not like I won't make it to town tomorrow; I'm definitely close enough now to make it to town tomorrow. So then, what? What is this about?

I descend, take another quick break, and start the final climb, but by now nothing is working for me, mentally. Loud music is not working and the magic of fruit snacks is not working and as I near the top I am suddenly filled with a hot and inexplicable rage. I hate hiking. I hate it I hate it. I hate everyone who is faster than me, who can cover these same miles in so much less time with many more breaks. I hate that this is the life I chose, that everyone I know is making babies and buying houses and publishing books, and I'm... what? Hiking myself into the ground in 30+ mph wind to reach some arbitrary stopping point for the day, for absolutely no fucking reason? The existential crisis has returned.

I stand at the top, finished with the final climb, staring at the massive descent to come, furious that I have to hike it. I stomp down the narrow switchbacks, one after the other after the other, all the way down to the creek, and then down a steep and terrifying rock slide where my rage is amplified by fear and all I can do is move slowly and carefully, muttering out loud to myself the whole time, an unending chorus of "oh fuck, you're doing great, don't look over the edge, you're doing great, oh fuck, don't look over the edge."

The diciest part is eventually behind me and I stomp down the talus and crisscross the creek and pick my way across a field of avalanche debris, scrambling over some of the fallen tree trunks, crawling under others, finally descending into the cool shade of the woods. The sun has begun to set now, and just as suddenly as it came my rage slips away. What does it matter if other people are making different choices with their lives? I worked so hard to build *this* life for myself, this exact life that I am so proud to claim as my own. Look at that little waterfall! Look at this good soft dirt beneath my feet! I cross the creek one more time, and there on the ground in front of me: small stones that another hiker has arranged into the shape of the number 400.

400 miles. I have now hiked 400 miles—the very life I chose for myself, indeed.

◁ ▷

Day 25

The harder the hiking the worse I sleep.

I wish this wasn't true, but apparently it is. 24 miles yesterday, with 11,000 ft of elevation change, and my body aches all night. I can't find a comfortable posi-tion, I flit in and out of strange dreams, and by dawn I feel like a fog has descended over my brain, like I am too groggy to even remember the order in which I usually put all the gear into my pack. Does the tent go on top? Where do I shove my rain coat? How can something that has been mindlessly easy for weeks all of the sudden stop making any sense?

I shrug it off, sticking everything in some haphazard place, not willing to expend the mental energy it would require to think it through. Who cares where the rain jacket is as long as I have it with me, right? All that really matters is that I hike.

It's cold this morning, my breath is a white cloud in front of my face, and since it's town day I let myself wear my leggings for the first few miles. I usually don't hike in my sleep clothes, trying to keep them dry and clean, but on town day I treat myself to the joy of not having cold legs in the early morning hours—a small but monumental delight.

The trail winds through the quiet forest, flat and damp with Elk Creek always rushing somewhere nearby, and I walk through cobwebs as the world wakes up. I boulder-hop across the creek, following the trail as it goes up high above the water, sunbeams bathing the surrounding mountains in soft amber light. Morning is my favorite time to hike, to let my mind wander over the well-worn grooves of my own heart and to explore new corners of it too, to think about love and loneliness and how we ever got lucky enough to deserve these leafy green aspen trees and purple wildflowers and the rushing sound of cold mountain creeks.

I move quickly through the woods, eventually crossing the train tracks where I've heard that if you wait long enough you can hitch a train ride into town. A train hitch! Imagine that. I sit on the ground near the tracks, my back up against the tall trunk of an old tree, eating snacks and mixing electrolyte fruit punch into my water bottle. It's all uphill from here, 5 miles of climbing to Molas Pass, and yet I am surprised to find that I don't dread it. I think about something my friend Carrot once said, about how when she first started hiking she dreaded the climbs, "but the endorphins of steep climbs are a thing without parallel, and that feeling you get upon reaching the top is a feeling to build one's entire life around."

Indeed.

So up I go for miles through the trees, one switchback after another after another, just switchbacking up into the sky, an endless forest with speckled light filtering down through the thick summer leaves. Eventually the trail opens up to a wide meadow, and off in the distance

Nicole Antoinette

192

I see that Gent is hiking toward me, down from the trailhead at Molas Pass where he must have parked the van. We cover the final miles together, reaching the van before noon where there is a gloriously cold bottle of orange juice waiting for me, followed by a quick ride into Silverton.

Silverton! My last resupply stop! 412 miles down, just 74 to go.

We park in front of a hostel with a sign that declares it used to be a brothel. Immediately upon check-in I charge up to our room and take what can only be called an orgasmic shower, a rebirthing shower, the hot water just pounding and streaming down my filthy skin, leaving me fresh and new and clean and sated. And I'm sure the brothel was fun but have you ever taken a 20-minute shower with perfect water pressure after 412 miles of hiking? My god.

In no time at all I've exploded my gear across the room, amazed yet again at how the contents of one small backpack can fill such a large surface area. Little bits of trash collect on the floor, the remnants of my food bag get dumped on the bed, and all the dirty clothes go into a pile for the wash. Laundry, I should definitely start doing laundry, but there is a place a few blocks away that serves funnel cakes—seriously just an entire restaurant that is dedicated solely to funnel cakes—and so of course we go, finding Milkshake and EFT on the street along the way, convincing them to come with us.

"I will buy everyone their own huge funnel cake," I say. "Come. This is happening."

The menu is surprisingly long (so many different toppings!) and Gent gets his with blueberries while I order mine with cinnamon, powdered sugar, and whipped cream. I don't pay any attention to what Milkshake and EFT order, as I am instead entirely focused on the person putting the raw dough into the big fryer, watching as it splutters and sizzles and fills the air with a maddeningly delicious smell.

Plates piled high with our fried dough concoctions, the four of us sit at a table out front, quickly abandoning normal conversation for the delightful silence of each devouring our own funnel cake one sloppy bite at a time.

Afterward Gent and I wander down the town's main street, poking around in the touristy gift shops until the soreness in my feet and my overall exhaustion is such that all I want is to be horizontal. I need to pick up my resupply box from the post office, and I need to wash my clothes, and I probably need to eat something other than deep friend sugary dough, but not now. Now I am going to rest. I am going to sprawl out across my soft hotel bed and try to somehow wrap my mind around the fact that I only have one section of this trail left—that if I can make it 74 more miles I will have truly actually done this thing. I will be a Colorado Trail thru-hiker.

◁ ▷

Day 26

I sleep deeply, mostly due to the dose of Benadryl I took last night, which always helps me sleep but leaves me feeling groggy and drugged come morning. Is it worth it? Restful sleep but a sluggish first few hours of the day? Maybe. I don't know.

I stretch under the covers, feeling all the places where my body has worked and worked and worked for the past 25 days. Gent climbs into bed with me and we cuddle, limbs all tangled together in a skin-on-skin love puddle that eventually gets interrupted by the deep rumbling and gurgling of my empty stomach.

We get dressed, walking hand in hand to the Lone Spur Cafe where I order a plate of truly enormous pancakes with butter and syrup, a side of extra crispy bacon, a glass of orange juice and a pot of tea. Full enough after breakfast to make good decisions, we head to the small grocery store in town where I wander the aisles and try to find something, anything that I will want to eat over the next few days, food to supplement what's in my resupply box from the post office, but as I picture the food in my box I notice how disgusted I feel by even just the thought of it—as if everything I forced myself to eat during those first 10-ish days of extreme nausea has now become the most unappealing food in the world.

So I buy some new flavors of cous cous, some string cheese, an apple and an avocado, a few bars of chocolate. Back at the hostel I arrange all the various food from the store and from my resupply box on the bed, trying to get excited about it. I am not excited about it though, and this bums me out until I remember that I only have to eat trail food for a few more days, because in a few more days I will have made it to Durango.

"You do not have to like this food," I tell myself sternly. "You don't have to be in the mood to eat it in order to eat it. This is just fuel to get you from here to Durango, that's all."

Soon I'm packed up and ready to go, and I say goodbye to EFT in the hostel lobby. He's staying in town for an extra day, so we won't see each other again.

"Where's Milkshake?" I ask. Milkshake is heading back to trail today, like me.

"At a restaurant?" EFT says, a question in his voice. Milkshake is maybe at a restaurant.

"Well tell him to hike fast and catch up," I say.

It's noon by the time Gent drops me off at Molas Pass, and as I take my first few steps away from the trailhead I am bursting with anticipation for the final days of this adventure. It feels real now, the end I couldn't conceive of, not when we first started back in Denver, not when Gent quit, not when Bugbite quit, not when I hiked myself into the ground to outrun a lightning storm, not when I froze my water filter, not even yesterday as I climbed and climbed toward the road that would take me into Silverton. But now, now I am in the final section of this trail. A victory lap, so to speak. *Oh my god*, I think, *I am actually going to be able to hike this hike!*

This thought supercharges my morale, and so even though the trail goes up for the first few miles I feel strong, fresh, born to do this. I climb away from Silverton, the trail running parallel to the many mountain peaks, my body just a little speck surrounded by huge clouds of all shapes, tall thick trees, burnt red dirt, rust orange rock slabs, water flowing everywhere. Storms rage over the various ridges in what seems like every single direction, lightning and thunder that is always just far enough away that I stay safe. As I hike I feel protected, cared for, watched over, loved.

I get up and over the day's high point, descend back into the trees with the cool breeze and my salty snacks, playfully rock hopping across stream after stream, water splashing all over my legs. Scenery wise I feel like this is the prettiest day so far—my favorite terrain, nonstop views that must be straight from the pages of some outdoor fairytale, and so I hike 10 miles, 12 miles, 15 miles, stopping briefly for only the shortest of breaks, too fired up about what might be around the next bend (and the next and the next!) to sit and rest for longer than a few minutes at a time.

By late afternoon I feel the sudden pressure in my gut that means I need to find a place to shit and I need to find it *now*, but luckily there is a grove of trees nearby, just far enough away from the trail for me to be mostly hidden from view, and I rush there as I experience the revenge of yesterday's funnel cake.

I climb for another hour or so after that, feeling much better, surprised that there are no other hikers to be seen. I keep expecting Milkshake to catch me but he

doesn't, and at 6:40pm, even though there's still another hour of daylight left, I decide to stop. I've hiked
18 miles since noon and that is enough. Besides, I love
this little flat spot on the wooded ridge and I want to
camp here. So I pitch my tent, change into my warm
sleep clothes, zip up my puffy jacket, and watch the
orange of the setting sun as it kisses the mountains
through the trees.

I sit cross-legged outside of my tent and eat lots of
cookies; my body feels good, my morale is still high, and
I even find that after 26 days I am finally fit enough to
blow up my sleeping pad at this high elevation without
getting dizzy—a true moment of glory indeed.

I lay the inflated pad down in the center of my tent,
sleeping bag fluffed up on top, and crawl inside my
backcountry nest. I watch through the mesh as darkness descends, as lightning breaks out above the ridge
across from me, bright and sharp against the night
sky. The storm will be over here soon, I think, but no
matter. I am warm and safe, I am eating my bars of
chocolate, I am tucked into the trees, all of my gear
placed just so inside the tent exactly the way I like it,
and I am prepared to wait out any storm that wants to
dance around me tonight.

◁ ▷

Day 27

The storm comes and goes throughout the night, thrashing wind, pouring rain, lightning that pierces the otherwise dark sky. I lay awake listening, falling back asleep each time it dies down, up for good at 6:30am. I pop my head out of my tent and am greeted by a chilly morning, clouds cleared away by the rain, sun beginning its move across the sky. I pack my things away quickly; I am ready to *hike*.

I'm just over 56 miles away from Durango now, and I feel a sort of wild energy pulsing inside of me, urging me to open myself up and push and push, really see what I can do. So often I am afraid of pushing too hard, of getting injured, of burning out, but the gift of being so close to the end is that it makes me brave enough to take some risks with my body, to be a little reckless with how high I set the bar and how seriously I try to reach it.

The trail takes me across ridges and into the vibrant forest again and again this morning, winding upward toward Blackhawk Pass. I'm so hungry today, eating every hour, my inner furnace burning hot and needy. The final climb up to the top of the pass feels hard, and I remind myself that of course it's hard—just because I am stronger doesn't make the thing easy, it simply means that I am more able to do it.

So I climb and I sweat, trekking poles tapping against the hard-packed dirt with every step. The top of the pass, when I eventually get there, is achingly beautiful, surrounded by stacks of mountains with their chunky bands of red rock, and I sit and stare and feel like I never ever want to leave. 10 minutes, 20 minutes, letting my eyes roam across every inch of land that I can see.

It's 11:30am now, and I reluctantly start descending down the other side, back into the trees, stopping at the rushing creek to fill up on water for the 13-mile dry stretch ahead. I take a liter and a half, which probably isn't enough, but I have gotten so lazy about water on this trail. I love my light little pack! Water is so heavy! So I'll be thirsty for a while, so what. I'm tough.

So I hike and hike, rationing the water as afternoon comes and I find myself on a series of exposed ridges in the harsh sun, no shade, and by 2pm my high morning morale has evaporated and this all starts to feel like an unbearable grind.

I lay down on the ground, eyes closed against the brightness of the sun, eating gummy candy. That helps.

When I stand up again I decide to turn on a podcast, the first thing I've listened to all day, and that helps too—distraction as self-care.

It's okay that it feels like a grind right now, I tell myself. You've been hiking for 7+ hours straight and sometimes even the things we love the very most feel like work.

So I listen to podcasts one after the other, take lots of short breaks, eat more candy, drink all of my water. It's 5:30pm by the time I reach Deer Creek, and I climb down the steep slope a little ways to fill up from the trickle of water that remains this late in the summer, evaluating my options for the night as I wait and wait for the water bottle to be full.

There are a few tents pitched near here. Should I stay? Should I camp here too? It's pretty early. But I've already done 25.4 miles. And yet I feel like I can do more. But the next few miles of trail are all climbing. Will that be awful? What if it takes until after dark to find a good flat spot for my tent? I should stay here, right?

Fuck it, I think, let's see what else I've got.

So I stash the water bottle away, and go. Up up up into the evening, 26 miles, 27 miles, 28 miles. The decision to push myself has given me the energy I need to push myself, a sort of positive feedback loop in which I keep asking myself what all this strength is even for, if not this.

So I keep going, and it feels so good to push, to not be so cautious, so afraid of getting injured like Gent and Bugbite. *You are not going to hurt yourself*, I repeat as I hike. *You are not, you are not, you are not.*

I reach the top of the climb at 7:15pm, walking along a ridge that looks out over an enormous expanse of mountains. The sun is setting, rich orange light spreading out across the sky as I find a little flat spot amongst the few sparse and spindly trees. I pitch my tent, legs throbbing as I do some quick calculations and realize I just hiked almost 30 miles.

Damn, I think. What if I actually *can* do mileage like this. What if I can do more than I ever imagined.

◁ ▷

Day 28

There's a deer outside my tent for most of the night, taking care of whatever important business a deer has to do from 11pm onward. I clap my hands loudly, scare it away, but it comes right back. More clapping, the deer darts away again, but it always comes back.

And so I sleep fitfully, body zinging in pain from yesterday's outrageous increase in mileage, and yet when sunrise blooms across the sky it is so beautiful that I forget to be tired. I forget to be in pain. I just scramble out of my tent, pulling on my puffy in the cold morning air, going right over to the edge of the ridge to watch the colors of the waking world illuminate in front of my eyes.

Once the sun is fully up I begin to pack my tent away. Right here, as I stand in this spot, I am 27 miles from the end of the trail. Hiking 27 miles immediately after hiking 30 miles feels pretty stupid, especially given that those 27 miles include 3,200 feet of climbing and 7,900 feet of descending. Seventy nine *hundred* feet. Will I even have knees left after that? Shouldn't I have started earlier in the morning if I wanted to go all the way?

You do not have to decide now, I tell myself. Just go one mile at a time.

So I finish packing up and I hike out, and almost straight away I am gasping for breath on the steep steep trail. I stop once to take my jacket off, again to take my mittens off, sweating as I move upward while I also try to keep my footing on the various talus fields along the way.

The talus slows me down, way down, and I panic as I do the math on my current pace. No way I can make it to Durango today if I keep moving this slowly. No way, no way. I fret about this incessantly as I climb up one little peak, two peaks, three peaks, worrying all the while.

Finally, on the descent down to the lake, I stop myself mid-stride and look around. I mean I *really* look around, at the jagged mountains, the vibrant green trees, the sunlight glinting off the deep blue of the water below, and I realize that my obsession with whether or not I'll be able to finish this hike today is ruining the magic of it. Who cares if I finish today? If it's not today it will definitely be tomorrow. This is not a race. I am not competing against the clock or against any other hikers or even against myself. I came out to the Colorado Trail to see if this thing I thought I wanted three years ago—this lifestyle that I got divorced for and moved into a van for and uprooted my life for, this dream that I needed to break my own heart in order to be able to chase—I came out here to see if it was real. If after all of that and after a year and a half of living through a pandemic, if I still wanted it. If a future of being able to drop everything and go into the mountains for months at a time was worth what I would be continually giving up in terms of income stability and feeling rooted in a home community and whatever else I might have to sacrifice in order to have it.

I wanted that vision enough to try, that's why I started this hike 28 days ago. And I wanted it enough to keep going when my partner quit and then again when my friend quit. I wanted it enough to stay out here even when staying out here was the less convenient option.

Oh my god, I realize. I *want* this. Not just for today or for a few weeks. I want this forever. I want to do it with my loved ones and I want to do it alone. I am so good at being alone now! *I want this, I want this, I want this.*

And so I slow down. I stop panicking about when I will make it to Durango. I let my breath deepen and expand, imagining that by doing so I can call back all of the energy I have allowed to leak out through my worries this morning. I pull all of this energy back into myself, into my heart and my bones and my blood. I will get there when I get there, and I will give myself the gift of experiencing it completely along the way.

Down at the lake I stop for a quick snack, a few sips of water, and then I follow the trail for miles and miles, just me and my heavy legs and my light light heart. I hike 5 miles, 8 miles, 10 miles, descending a steep talus ridge with tiny careful steps, descending through explosions of wildflowers, air thick with their ripe floral scent. I check my phone a few times, keeping an eye on the clock, but eventually I manage to stop doing that as well, to keep my phone zipped away in my fanny pack as I move through the warm humid air, my skin slick with sweat as I get lower and lower in elevation.

I reach Junction Creek, where I spread out on my little foam pad, shoes and socks off, sitting down to drink electrolyte fruit punch while I surround myself with an array of everything that still remains in my food bag— Goldfish and mint Milano cookies and string cheese and peanuts and barbecue flavored potato chips.

As I eat, I look at the map. This is it, I realize, the moment when I do actually need to decide whether or not I'm going all the way tonight, because this is the last reliable water source between here and the terminus. It's early afternoon now, and I have hiked 12.5 miles. Can I hike 14.5 more?

I close my eyes, slowing my breathing and tunneling as deep as I can into myself, down into the place where the truth resides. What do you want to do, I ask myself.

Go.

I feel the answer as it reverberates out from my own center. *I want to go.*

I smile, packing away the last of the snacks, filling up only as much water as I'll need to finish this hike without being terribly thirsty. There's only one climb left, a little more than 4 miles up and away from the creek, and after that it's downhill almost all the way.

You can do this, I tell myself. But as I say the words I realize that I don't need the pep talk, not anymore. Of course I can do this, I've been doing it all along.

So I shoulder my pack and I start to climb, surprised to find that even in my exhausted state that it is not nearly as hard as I expected. It's almost... easy? Effortless? Because the reality is that I've got over 400 miles in my legs right now and there is very little that these legs cannot do.

I climb among the leafy aspen trees, the distinctive markings in their white bark keeping me company until I reach the top, where there is enough cell service to call Gent and tell him when to meet me, tell him that I am now only 10 miles from the end.

I cry as I hike, loud wrenching sobs, and the release I get as the tears stream down my face is enough to make me cry even harder, fatigue and joy mixing together as I try to understand what I have almost accomplished.

9 miles to go, 8 miles, 7 miles. I sit on a fallen log and eat the rest of my cookies. As I do a mountain biker comes by, stopping to wait for her son to catch up.

"Where are you headed today?" she asks, dirt streaks and a big smile on her face, the same look I am probably wearing on mine.

"Durango!" I say, just as her young son pulls up.

"And where did you start?" she asks.

"Today you mean? Or like, in general?"

"Both?"

"Well," I say, delighted that these next words are true, "last night I camped about 20 miles back, and on August 1st I started in Denver."

"Oh fuck," she says.

"Mom!" her son yells. "We aren't allowed to use that word!" He looks both astonished and highly scandalized as his stare bounces quickly from his mom to me and back again.

"Honey," she says, "sometimes that word is the only one that will work."

I laugh, and she laughs, and her son continues to stare at us both, utterly bewildered.

"You're finishing today aren't you?" she says.

"Yes," I tell her. "I am 7 miles away from completing this whole fucking hike."

She rides away after that, cackling as her son is right on her wheel, trying to get her to explain the specifics of when it is okay to say "fuck" and what has to be true for *him* to be able to say it too, and I find myself laughing as well, even long after they have pulled away.

7 more miles. Only 7 more miles to go.

And yet 7 miles is not zero miles, a fact that I am reminded of as I take a few steps and immediately feel the cumulative oppressive forces of the heat and of being sleep deprived and of having already hiked 50 miles since yesterday morning. I hike a half mile, another half mile, and another half mile after that. I'm moving in a weirdly jerky way now, as if my gait has broken down to try and compensate for whichever muscles in my legs are the most depleted. I can feel myself wobbling as I walk, a sort of unsteady shuffling movement where I'm barely picking my feet up off the ground, nothing at all like the fresh and pretty stride I had way back at the start of this hike.

So you'll do it ugly, I think, the phrase rushing into my mind with the force of a command. *Do it ugly.* Because if that's all you've got it will have to be enough.

With four miles to go I reach a wooden bench that's right out near the edge of the mountainside. I drop my things and lay down, back flat against the warm hard stone, eyes closed, willing myself to be able to keep going.

"Oh hey," I hear from just down the trail, my eyes popping open in surprise. It's Gent!

"What are you doing here?" I ask, sitting up so fast I give myself a head rush. "This will be 8 miles round trip for you—are you sure your achilles is up for that?"

"I was getting restless waiting," he says. "I just love you so much and I am so proud of you and I didn't want to miss any more of this hike than I absolutely had to."

He sits next to me on the bench and I rest my head against his shoulder.

"I love you too," I say. "Thank you for coming for me."

"Always," he says. And then, after a beat, "Let's go, Tink. It's time for you to finish this thing."

I grab my pack and my trekking poles, falling in line behind him on the narrow trail. I am absolutely gassed now, my internal tank running on the barest of fumes, and so I imagine a fuel line stretching from my chest to Gent's back, pretending that his energy is my energy too.

"Three more miles," he says a half hour later.

We hike and hike, the trees and the dirt and the sky all blurring together into a tunnel through which I somehow continue to push myself.

"Two miles," I whisper.

And then, soon, "one more mile."

"There it is!" I yell, spotting the big sign at the trail-head as we come around the final bend—the southern terminus of the Colorado Trail.

I place both palms against it when I get there, laughing and crying and unable to stop thinking about what Anne Lamott said, that there are only three prayers we ever need: *help, thanks, wow*, and how I used every single one of those prayers on every single day of this hike, and in doing so these 491 miles of 'help, thanks, wow' have connected me back to myself in a way that I didn't know I so desperately needed.

I step away from the sign, running over to hug Gent who has given me some space to have this celebratory moment all to myself.

"Thank you," I say, and I realize that I am saying it to him, yes, but maybe even more so I am saying it to myself. I am acknowledging that I did not leave my own side, not once during this whole hike, not when I was sad and lonely, not when I was in pain, not when I was exhausted, not ever.

And because of that, because I stayed, because I knew that staying was what I owed to myself, I have made it here, not just to the end of the trail but to that place deep inside of myself where if I am really lucky, once in a while I find that I can reach out and touch the most divine part of what it means to be human.

Acknowledgments

To Gent, for everything, always.

To Carrot, for writing the book that first got me into long-distance hiking back in 2016. *Thru Hiking Will Break Your Heart*, indeed.

To my Word Camp and Get Shit Done Club pals, this book only exists because of all the many hours we spent in digital community together, unabashedly supporting each other's creative dreams.

To Steve Kuhn and Sarah Lahay, who designed the book cover and did the interior layout, respectively. It was such a pleasure to collaborate with you both! Thank you for making it so that people can hold these words in their hands.

And to you, dear reader, for reliving this journey with me. I hope it nudges you to take whatever kind of leap your own heart most desires.

About the Author

Nicole Antoinette is a writer and long-distance hiker who is totally obsessed with the transformative power of honest conversations.

She is forever thinking about the question of how we can close the gap between what we say we want and what we actually do, all while having fun and being kind and gentle to ourselves along the way.

You can learn more about Nicole and her work at:
nicoleantoinette.com

Milton Keynes UK
Ingram Content Group UK Ltd.
UKHW011945010124
435297UK00004B/387